English as a Foreign Language

Also by R. A. Close

The New English Grammar Parts 1 *and* 2
(Allen & Unwin 1964)

The New English Grammar Parts 3 *and* 4
(Allen & Unwin 1968)

The English We Use
(Longman 1961, revised 1971)

The English We Use for Science
(Longman 1965)

Prepositions
(Longman 1967)

The Future
(Longman 1970)

A University Grammar of English Workbook
(Longman 1974)

A Reference Grammar for Students of English
(Longman 1975)

English Grammatical Structure
(with L. G. Alexander, W. Stannard
Allen and R. O'Neill)
(Longman 1975)

English as a Foreign Language

Its Constant Grammatical Problems

Its Constant Grammatical Problems

Third Edition

R. A. CLOSE

Research Fellow, University College, London

PE
1128
.C66
1981

London
GEORGE ALLEN & UNWIN
Boston   Sydney

First published in 1962
Sixth impression 1974
Second edition 1977
Second impression 1978
Third edition 1981

40 Museum Street, London WC1A 1LU

© George Allen & Unwin (Publishers) Ltd, 1976, 1977, 1981

British Library Cataloguing in Publication Data

Close, Reginald Arthur
    English as a foreign language. – 3rd ed.
    1. English language – Text-books for foreigners
    I. Title
    428′.2′4   PE1128

ISBN 0–04–425025–8

Printed in Great Britain
in 10 point Times Roman type
at Unwin Brothers Limited
The Gresham Press, Old Woking, Surrey

PREFACE

I offer two reasons for producing a third edition of this book only three years after the appearance of the second. One is that I have found widespread confusion amongst teachers and students about the role that grammar has to play now that notional syllabuses and the communicative approach to language teaching have caused yet another revolution in the English language teaching world. A second reason is that *English as a Foreign Language* continues to be used as a standard textbook in many parts of the world, and some of its readers have kindly supplied me with ideas for further improvement.

The British and other European scholars who have developed the idea of notional syllabuses and have advocated a communicative approach have thereby made a very significant contribution to language teaching. However, although those ideas needed emphasis and have met with remarkable success, they are not entirely new. As a teacher of English and a learner of several other tongues, I, like many of my professional colleagues, have always been conscious of the need to use a language for definite purposes and to convey specific meanings through it. Many of the *notions* referred to in recent literature were expressed by the late Dr I. A. Richards in the draft of a textbook on which he kindly asked me to comment when he was working in Peking, and I in Shanghai, as long ago as 1937. That accounts for my acknowledgement of I. A. Richards's influence, mentioned in all three editions of the present book. I found his reference to certain concepts—notably those related to space, time, dimension, motion, direction, location, events and processes—invaluable when I was thinking out the original version of *English as a Foreign Language*. Similarly, by working with H. J. Uldall, I learnt the importance of distinguishing between verbs that referred to action taking place at a point of time and those referring to activities continuing throughout a *period* of time: hence my expression of indebtedness to him also. Notions of that kind have helped me towards a solution of grammatical problems: they should be distinguished from functions—such as asking for information, making requests, giving advice, and so on—which are performed through a variety of grammatical constructions.

What has disturbed many teachers is the fear that notional syllabuses and the communicative approach mean excluding grammar from the curriculum. True, protagonists of this new—or newly-emphasized—methodology, have drawn attention to the comparative futility (for all except dedicated grammarians) of the

7

learner's mastering grammatical structures for their own sake and of constructing perfectly grammatical sentences without being able to say what he wants or has to say at the moment when he feels compelled to say it. But experts on the new methodology had no intention of excluding grammar from the curriculum. D. A. Wilkins, author of *Notional Syllabuses* (Wilkins, 1976) states, on page 19 of his book, ' . . . the notional syllabuses can ensure that the most important grammatical forms are intended'. *The Threshold Level*, by J. A. Van Ek (1975), and *A Communicative Grammar of English* by G. Leech and Jan Svartvik (1975), both key books in this context, each contains an indispensable grammatical compendium (see list of Further Reading on p. 205). There would be no sense in excluding grammar from the curriculum: the many functions that English can perform, and the many ways of communicating in our language, all more or less demand the application of those conventions that constitute its grammar. In any case, the subject of this book is not syllabuses and curricula, but the grammatical problems which arise wherever English, as a foreign language, is studied and taught.

In this third edition, I have added a chapter on notions and functions, not only to illustrate explanations that were in the book already, but also to take into account the important work that has been published on those subjects in the last few years. I have also taken advantage of the advice of readers by making what I hope are minor improvements; by re-writing much of the first chapter; by providing more examples and by adding to the list of books for further reading.

The original title of the book, *English as a Foreign Language* has been retained, if only because it is under that name that the work has become widely known (though, according to more than one reader, not widely enough). I hope that the sub-title, *Its Constant Grammatical Problems*, will help to indicate that this is not a complete grammar, but a grammar's companion, which has been designed to deal with difficulties that I have found, in my fairly long experience, to cause trouble everywhere, and whatever methodology happens to be currently favoured.

This book was written primarily for teachers and advanced students for whom English is a foreign language. It has proved welcome not only to them, but also to those 'young graduates' (to quote Professor E. W. Hawkins, Director of the Language Teaching Centre at the University of York) 'trained in our schools and attracted abroad to teach English, whose grammar . . . they have not begun to explore'.

May I conclude with a word of advice to those who think of using this book? It is not intended to be consulted in the way in which we look up isolated words in a dictionary. There are lines of argument running through it, and there are patterns, applicable to one grammatical problem, which can be applied, with variations, to a different problem dealt with in a later chapter. I have made a few cross-references; but I know that readers are apt to be irritated by constant cross-reference, which they find disturbs their train of thought. In any case, I have always thought of this book as one to be read through, chapter by chapter; and reading it first in that way will, I think, prove more helpful than picking pieces of information out of their full context.

ACKNOWLEDGEMENTS

It was the famous head of this publishing house, Sir Stanley Unwin, who insisted that I write this book. When it was finally out, he expressed his approval in the words: 'This will be revised by my successors and yours.' Sir Stanley died in 1968, aged 83. Dedicating this revision to his memory, I also express my gratitude to those of his successors who have helped fulfil his prediction thus far.

The original work bore the influence of Dr I. A. Richards, whom I first met in China and who was an immense help to me in analysing problems of English as seen from the other side of the globe. Other influences came from Mr H. J. Uldall (of the School of the great Otto Jespersen of Copenhagen) with whom I worked at the Institute of English Studies in Athens; and members of the Prague School who were such faithful friends to me when I was in Czechoslovakia from 1946 to 1950.

In this revision, I have gladly taken advantage of criticisms made by that elder statesman among European grammarians of English, Professor R. W. Zandvoort of Groningen, in his very encouraging review in *English Studies* (Amsterdam); and by Professor S. Pit Corder, of Edinburgh, in *The Modern Language Review*. I have made use of equally helpful suggestions from Professor Bruce Pattison, of the Institute of Education, University of London; by Professor Sidney Greenbaum of the University of Wisconsin-Milwaukee; and by Professor Wolf-Dietrich Bald of the Institut für Anglistik at Aachen. I am indebted to other scholars, notably Professor Henri Adamczewski and Inspecteur Général Denis Girard, of Paris, who have urged me not to abandon 'insights' that seem to have given the original book its appeal.

In the three editions, I have benefited from the enlightened and scholarly enthusiasm of my good friend Dr A. H. King, formerly of the British Council, now Professor of English at the Brigham Young University, Utah. Above all, from the start of this whole enterprise I have had the enormous advantage of being able to draw on the wealth of ideas, brilliantly expressed in conversations, at meetings, lectures and seminars, and in his writings, by Professor Randolph Quirk, Director of the Survey of English Usage at University College, London.

I mention these scholars only to acknowledge my debt to them, and I trust I have not misinterpreted any of their work in a book written by a teacher of English for his fellow-teachers and his students.

University College, London   R. A. C.

CONTENTS

CONVENTIONS

Oblique strokes (/. . . /) mark phonetic transcription.

A vertical line before a word or a syllable indicates that that word or syllable is stressed, as in *The dis'tinguished 'president*.

An asterisk before a word, phrase or sentence means that what follows is unacceptable.

The symbol *v* = in contrast with.

        i.e. = that is; e.g. = for example;
        c.p. = compare.

CHAPTER 1

Rules in English Grammar

Has English a Grammar? If it has, what are its Rules?

1 It has often been said that English has no grammar, or that, if it has, there are no rules in it. English has indeed very few of the kind of inflections, on the end of nouns and verbs, that play such an important part in the grammar of many other languages. English adjectives have no inflections at all, apart from the *-er* and *-est* of short words like *longer* and *longest*. There are still, in the nineteen-eighties, writers of English grammar who try to present their subject on the same model as, say, Latin, French or German, and produce paradigms like:

I play	we play
you play	you play
he, she, it plays	they play

But, except for *plays*, the form of the verb in the Present Tense remains unchanged; while in the Past Tense, *I played* etc., the form of the verb is invariable. Yet over half a century ago, the great Danish grammarian, Otto Jespersen, wrote, ' . . . it is impossible to see the use of such paradigms as are found in many English grammars . . . ' (*The Philosophy of Grammar* 1924). We can accurately predict the whole 'conjugation' of every verb in modern English from a small set of rules and a fixed list of irregularities (see, for example, *A Reference Grammar for Students of English* Longman, 1975, sections 1.16–1.20). Nor has English grammar a place for gender in nouns. *Cow* is not 'feminine gender' as opposed to the 'masculine' *bull*. *Cow* and *bull* are two separate words, one referring to a female of a species of animal, the other to the male. Both words can be preceded by the same set of determiners, e.g. *a, any, each, either, every, my, the, this, that*, etc., each of which has one form only.

2 English grammar is chiefly a system of syntax that decides the order and patterns in which words are arranged in sentences. The

13

system works largely with the help of what are called grammatical or structural words—auxiliary verbs, determiners, pronouns, prepositions and conjunctions. These words form a 'closed set', i.e. there is a fixed number of them and new members are not admitted.

3   It is true that English grammar has no rules established for it by any authority. Individual grammarians have stated their own opinions and preferences and have made up their own body of rules. Some, like H. W. Fowler (*Modern English Usage*, revised by Sir Ernest Gowers, 1965), have been and are still regarded with the greatest respect, and have helped to keep usage stable. Others are not so reliable. However, according to present-day thinking there are rules in English grammar that can be accurately formulated from the observation and analysis of a large number of examples of widely accepted educated usage. The rules so formulated can account for the way in which competent users of the language produce original acceptable utterances, sentences, speeches and written texts.

4   In these days, it is also often said that, while grammatical rules for English can be found, to conform to them is not so important as to 'communicate'. Therefore teachers are tempted to let their students express themselves freely without worrying whether the results are grammatical or not. Such an attitude could not merely lead to a degree of carelessness which I, for one, would find repugnant, but it might eventually end in the breakdown of a highly developed language as a communicative medium. Long before such a state of chaos was reached, the lack of attraction in slipshod speech and writing would have deprived efforts to communicate of much of their potential effect. Effective communication depends very largely on a complex set of conventions which both speaker and hearer, writer and reader, have to follow and understand. We can, admittedly, communicate by isolated words and phrases, as in *Fire, Fire, On the first floor!* Yet even that phrase *on the first floor* is constructed in accordance with the English grammatical system. If communication is our aim—and with any reasonable speaker and writer it normally is—then the fact remains that communication can generally be achieved most efficiently by means of a grammatical sentence or by a series of such sentences logically related.

Grammar as Fact

5   English grammar is first and foremost a matter of fact. We say *one man*, *two men*; *write*, *wrote*, *written*; *he may drive*, *he wants to* *drive, no one will stop him driving.* Whoever learns English must accept such forms and constructions as facts, and must develop the habit of using them in appropriate situations. Helping us to observe and remember the facts, the linguist arranges them methodically and draws general rules from them when he can. Perhaps he can explain historically how they came to be what they are. But the facts remain, decided for us. *Men* or *I wrote* or *he wants to* is 'right'; **mans, *I writed, *he mays to* are 'wrong': there we have no choice.

Grammar as a Question of Choice

6 Often in speaking and writing English we have a choice of forms, each of which by itself is correct. *'How shall I know if I do choose the right?'* asks the Prince of Morocco in Shakespeare's *Merchant of Venice*. There are three ways of deciding what to select. We can let ourselves be guided by our own experience of the language—experience gained by reading or from hearing the language naturally spoken. Secondly, we can rely for an answer on somebody who knows intuitively the right thing to say (though he may not be able to explain why it is right). Thirdly, we can find a solution in a grammar book which is concerned not so much with facts as with subtle distinctions of thought, personal and inter-personal attitudes, and individual points of view. Notice I say 'not *so much* with facts'. There is always an element of fact in these problems—the exact words and phrases uttered (the linguistic facts) and the circumstances in which they were used (the non-linguistic facts). What turns these questions into problems is the element of choice and of subtle distinction which the student, learning English as foreign speech, may fail to appreciate or even to see.

7 It is this aspect of English grammar that the non-native speaker of the language finds most worrying. When to use or omit *the* or *a*; whether to say *I write* or *I'm writing, have written* or *wrote*; how to use *have been writing* and *had been writing*; what tenses to use with *if* or *since*; how to use *can, may, could, would, should, might, must*; whether to put the infinitive or the part of the verb ending in *-ing*; which preposition it is to be; whether to say *some* or *any, each* or *every*; where in a sentence to put adverbs; which of the four words *say, tell, explain, show* could fill the gap in *Please . . . me how this works*: these problems and others like them have been, and still are, very common in the learning of English as a foreign language. (I base this statement not only on my own experience, of over forty years, of English teaching in various parts of the world, but also on reports

on the work of candidates in the English language paper compiled
by the University of Cambridge Local Examinations Syndicate.

8 Failure to master these distinctions may not always cause
misunderstanding. You can often make your meaning clear without
using *the* or *a* at all (see **97**). Are they then superfluous, or have they
roots that go deep into the thought of English speakers? To Henry
Sweet (*New English Grammar*, Part 1, Section 587, 1891), 'distinctions
of verb-tense, and the use of prepositions and of verbal-groups (i.e.
groups of words whose nucleus is an infinitive, participle or gerund)
. . . are . . . highly developed in English, and are part of the genius of
the language.' In the passage from which that quotation was drawn,
Sweet was explaining how tense-forms and 'verbal-groups' in English
take the place of the subjunctive in certain other languages. He went
on to say, 'The faculty by which we instinctively know whether a
certain form or construction is in accordance with the genius of the
language or not is called "the linguistic sense". This faculty is
naturally more highly developed in some people than in others; but it
can always be strengthened by training, and the first business of
grammar is to cultivate it as far as possible.'

9 Sweet had in mind readers for whom English was a mother-
tongue. Now the problems of English grammar that bewilder the
non-native speaker of English most, rarely seem to bother the
native speaker at all. The latter may fumble over tense-forms and
prepositions as a child, and may be weak in his command of the
language in other respects. Yet unconsciously he gets to know what
satisfies the 'genius' of his tongue. If his linguistic sense is keen, as
a good writer's is, he will use words and constructions with precision.
If it is dull, he will use them erratically, in blind obedience to custom
and habit. But whether his own usage is deliberate, precise and
consistent, or automatic, haphazard and confused, what makes him
decide to use *the*, *a*, or neither, or to choose one tense rather than
another, may be as much as a mystery to him—if he ever thought
about it—as it is to the non-native learner. I assume that the readers
of this book are among the many who are, or will be, obliged to
think about it.

10 The student can ultimately acquire this 'faculty' through the
constant reading of interesting, well-written English, or by being
steeped for years in a cultivated English-speaking atmosphere. He
stands a good chance of developing it if he is taught by men and
women whose vision of the distinctions of thought involved is clear,

and who can illustrate the distinctions effectively through vivid, memorable examples. It is very unlikely that he could acquire the faculty by being given abstract explanations first. Accurate statements about these problems are often particularly difficult to formulate, even for the trained linguist. They are far harder for the student to understand if he has not already had the experience of the distinctions of thought in genuine examples within a proper context.

11   We can therefore imagine English grammar as a solid core of linguistic facts (*men, wrote, he wants to drive*) surrounded by a more nebulous area in which linguistic facts (*I wrote, I have written*) are often involved with subtle distinctions of thought, personal attitudes and points of view, as well as with non-linguistic facts, such as the particular circumstances in which certain words were uttered, thus:

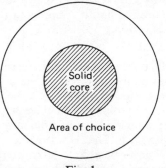

Fig. 1

A reasonable first aim in learning the grammar would be to master the solid core by learning the facts, whether one commits them to memory consciously or not. Mastering the rest of the grammar— which means learning to make the right choice—can only come from hearing, seeing, imitating and practising well-chosen examples in meaningful contexts—above all from constantly reading the language, and attentively listening to it well-spoken. Abstract explanations will then help. But for explanations to help they must be accurate, strictly in accordance with genuine acceptable usage, and as clear as possible.

12   The Appendix on page 204 summarises the contents of the 'solid core'. 'The rest', the area in which one has to learn to make the right choice, is the main subject of this book.

The Value of Rules

13   In the 'solid core' of fact, it is comparatively easy to formulate rules; though it is not quite so simple as we sometimes imagine. Many people, asked to state a rule for forming the plural of nouns in English, would say, 'Oh, just add *s* to the singular.' But that is not all the story: it ignores certain aspects of the spelling, which can be covered if the rule is stated more fully, and ignores the important matter of pronunciation. Add the sound *s* to the singular, *eye*, and you get *ice*. The plural of such a common noun as *nose* requires not only an *s* but also an extra syllable. Nevertheless, about the 'solid core' the linguist can—by taking into account all the relevant facts— fairly easily draw up a series of statements which will serve as reliable rules for our own use of the language. Even these rules, however, may have to be learnt in instalments; and the important thing is not that they should be learnt in the abstract but that the learner should acquire the habit of applying them automatically in real acts of communication.

14   In the more difficult area of choice there are very few conclusions that the linguist can easily draw. 'Give me a simple rule for using the articles, or the tenses' is asking for the impossible. Usually, teachers deal with these problems of choice step by step through the application of over-simplified 'rules' that are easily teachable but are only a part of the truth. That is a sensible thing to do, especially with pupils who will never be able to learn more than the rudiments of English. Unfortunately, half-truths are not valid for very long. I am not suggesting that we should abandon them, but that we should realise their limitations. Examples of their inadequacy are given below.

The Function of the Definite Article

15   'The definite article, "the", is used to indicate an object of which there is only one example present.' This is demonstrated in the classroom by contrasting *a chair, a book, a picture*—one of many chairs etc. in the room—with *the door*—the single door—*the floor, the ceiling*. But confusion in the learner's mind begins when the teacher adds *the table*, the one and only table, forgetting that in a previous lesson he had used that same article of furniture in ringing the changes on *This is a book*, thus: *This is a pen, This is a wall, This is a table*.

16 What is wrong? <u>The definite article is used to indicate a solitary example.</u> However, so is the indefinite article: it is quite correct to say *This is a table* when there is only one table to be seen. Furthermore, the definite article is used to indicate an object of which there are many examples present: in my mind's eye, I see a street full of houses and myself wearily walking from one to another, looking for the one to which I have been invited, and wondering, *Which is the house?* Finally, the definite article is often not used with an object of which there is only one example. If Shakespeare were present at this discussion, there would be an object of which only one example has ever existed; yet we do not say *the Shakespeare* until we imagine that there is more than one example and we wish to distinguish, let us say, *the Shakespeare we study* from *the Shakespeare his mother knew.*

17 *The Shakespeare we study* is in fact a good example of how the definite article in English functions, as we shall see in Chapter 3. Proper nouns, such as *Shakespeare*, are not normally preceded by an article in English. The definite article in English helps to identify one example of a concept, or more than one, and to isolate the identified object or objects from another or from others. In English, we do not feel the need for such a device with a proper noun: we feel that the name itself is enough to identify the object we have in mind. It is only when we begin to form more than one image of the object bearing that name, and wish to distinguish one of those images from another, that we use the article as a signal that we are making such a distinction.

The Present Continuous (or Progressive) and the Simple Present Tense

18 'The Present Continuous (or Progressive), as in *I'm writing*, is used for action performed at the time of speaking, the Simple Present, as in *I write*, for action performed habitually.' That is true in the examples *I am writing a book*, *Now you are reading it*, *I write a few hundred words every day* and in countless other cases. But the Simple Present is also used for action performed at the time of speaking. *I put my pen down at this point, get up and walk over to the window, thinking out what to say next.* I found myself saying those words quite naturally as I went through the motions.

19 In observing classes where English is being taught, and in reading manuscripts by prospective textbook writers, I am continually hearing and reading pronouncements such as the following: *We* *use the Present Continuous for what is happening now.* That is an example of an over-simplification which I would not call 'sensible'. It begs the question by using the Present Progressive (*is happening*) as a way of trying to explain the use of the Present Progressive itself; and it overlooks the fact that we could equally well say: *We use the Simple Present for what happens now*, as in *I used to write all my letters. Now I type them.* Furthermore, though that pronouncement would be true of *Now we are going to the University*, if the statement were made while we were actually on our way there, it would not apply to an example like *John is already eighteen: he is going to the University now*, when that information was imparted at a moment when John was at home oversleeping after a late night. We have therefore, in this paragraph, had two different examples of the use of the Present Progressive; and we shall find others later. The first is perhaps the most natural one to start with. But what is important about it as an initial presentation of the Present Progressive is not the relation between that construction and the word *now*, or an adverbial of similar meaning, but the association between the Present Progressive and a physical motion which one can see or feel in progress while that construction is being used. We need to establish the association, for example, between the utterance *I'm drawing a map of Africa* (in answer to the question *What are you doing?*) while our fingers and our pencil are moving towards the production of the map; or to establish the association between say, *John Cousins is skating beautifully*, spoken by a television commentator as we watch the skater moving to and fro across the television screen. In any case, with both the two different examples of the Progressive we have had in this paragraph, the essential feature is that an activity has already begun and has not yet ended when use of the Progressive is made.

20   Classroom English—the basis of much knowledge of English as a foreign language—is often artificial. It is unnatural when the teacher walks to the door, pulls the handle towards him and announces, 'I'm opening the door'. It would usually suit the words to the action on such an occasion more appropriately if the teacher said, 'I'm just going to open the door' or 'I've just opened the door'. In the same way, *I'm opening my book, Now I'm closing it, I'm switching on the light, I'm putting my pen on the desk*, as comments on what is happening now, would all be unnatural. Why? Because in such cases the teacher is commenting not on activity that has begun and is still in progress, but on a momentary act that could only be seen in a progressive state if performed very slowly or photographed by a slow-motion camera. If one wishes to demonstrate the Present Progressive while actually using that form, it would be more realistic to choose a verb referring to activity having duration, as in *Please be quiet for a minute or two, I'm writing an important letter;* or a verb referring to a series of momentary acts, as in *Hurry up or we'll be shut in. The caretaker is locking all the doors.*

21 When, in real life, does one have to comment on action at the time when it is being performed? Most of all, in these days, when describing an actual event for the benefit of a wireless audience or for television viewers; when showing someone how to operate a machine, or how to prepare and cook food; perhaps when performing a conjuring trick; when making formal declarations; and so on. In a radio commentary on present action, the Simple Present and the Present Progressive may occur with equal frequency. The following from a television commentary on a track race is typical; *They're moving up to their marks. They're off! No that was a false start. The starter motions them back.* In an observation of the constructions occurring in such commentaries, it was noted that the Simple Present was used almost entirely in an account of a football-match, the Present Progressive throughout a description of the Oxford and Cambridge boat-race. We cannot conclude from this either that the normal rules of English grammar do not apply to wireless commentaries, or that one set of rules applies to football-commentator's English, another to descriptions of university boat-races. The English of wireless commentators may be more alive and more naturally 'correct' than the artificially systematised language of English-teachers. The difference between the football-match and the boat-race is interesting and will be explained in **142**. As for other commentaries made at the time an action is performed, note: (*a*) *Now watch me: I switch on the current and stand back.* (*b*) *First, I make sure the gear is in neutral, and then I press the self-starter.* (*c*) *I pour the milk in slowly.* (*d*) *Look carefully: I cut the string once, and I cut it again.* (*e*) *I declare the meeting closed.* That, too, is natural English. To dismiss it as professional jargon, or as a special case for which some label like Instantaneous or Demonstrative Present must be found, will not help to solve our problems. Nor will it help if we argue that what the commentator really means is *Every time I do this, I* (*habitually*) *switch/stand back/make sure, etc.* He *may* mean that; but it is just as likely that he means *This is what I do now.*

22 The Simple Present is certainly used to relate habitual action.

But that does not entitle us to say that the distinction between the act performed at the present moment and the act performed repeatedly in present time is shown in English by a difference in tense-form, except incidentally in certain common types of usage. That distinction is an important one in languages, and it is made in English; but it is best shown in English by adverbial expressions or by the general context. The Simple Present is also used, as we have just seen, for an act performed now; and the Present Progressive can be used for habitual action: e.g. *You're always tapping on the table. Do stop it—it's a most annoying habit.* We must therefore look for other criteria in establishing the essential difference between these two tense-forms.

The Present Perfect

23 'The Present Perfect, *I have written*, is used when we are specially concerned with the present results of past action, when the evidence of past action lies before us.' There is much truth in this. *Hurray, I've found it. Here it is*, and many similar examples would prove the 'rule'. Yet even here we have not found a factor (apart from the form of the construction) which is common to all examples of the Present Perfect. When I tell you that *I have lived in China*, I am not necessarily concerned with present results at all, I am not in China now and have not lived there for many years. Evidence may exist of my having lived there, but that evidence would be there just the same if I said *I lived in China before the War*; and I could still say *I have lived in China* though every shred of evidence had disappeared.

24 'The Present Perfect is used for recent happenings, the Simple Past, *I wrote*, for less recent.' That would be true in some examples, e.g. *It's stopped raining.* But the converse is also true: *The post came five minutes ago. England has had its civil wars (the last was in the seventeenth century).*

The Present Perfect Continuous (or Progressive)

25 'The Present Perfect Continuous (or Progressive), as in *I've been writing*, is used for action begun in the past and still going on in the present.' The exact opposite of the last part of this 'rule' ('still going on in the present') is so often true that I doubt the value of teaching it even as a temporary aid. The 'rule' applies to such examples as *I've been writing this book for six weeks* (and am still writing it) and

You've been learning English for six years (and haven't stopped doing so). It does not apply to other examples, such as *Who's been sitting in my chair?* when whoever has been sitting in it has gone; or '*You've been working too hard*', said the doctor to his patient, motionless in bed.

The Past Continuous (or Progressive)

26 'The Past Continuous (or Progressive), as in *I was writing*, is used for an action which is interrupted by another action in the past.' This is part of the traditional dogma of European language teachers. It sometimes applies to English, but only incidentally and by no means invariably. In *I was writing when the bell rang*, an interruption is implied. In *The bell was still ringing but I worked on without noticing it* or in *Someone was taking notes all the time you were speaking*, what is interrupted by what? *I was writing steadily throughout the afternoon* suggests that I was not interrupted for a moment.

In a place, or at it?

27 'In referring to location, *in* is used with a capital city or town with a large number of inhabitants, *at* with a smaller place.' Insofar as this is true, it is a good example of the grammarian's prescription and of conventional usage. I have often found myself saying *in Edinburgh, in Prague, in Tokyo*, in conscious obedience to this 'rule', or to please such inhabitants of those great cities as might expect the rule to be observed for their benefit. Yet the 'rule' is not invariable. An aeroplane flying round the world can be said to stop *at Tokyo, at New Delhi, at Athens, at London*, on its way to New York; and we can say *in* the smallest of villages if that is the world we live in. But let us be careful not to make more rules out of these 'exceptions'. It is a fact (of which we can be certain) that we often use *at* with capital cities on air routes and *in* with villages when we are living in them; but a more fundamental point (of which admittedly we cannot be certain but which would make sense of both 'normal' and 'exceptional' usages) might be that we tend to associate *at* with what we imagine at the time of speaking to be a *point*, and *in* with what we imagine to be a *space*, as we shall see later.

28 The reader may come across other over-simplifications. He can always discover how far rules are inadequate by testing them against genuine and generally acceptable usage. Rules that break down under that test should not be regarded as axioms, but at best as temporary scaffolding poles which, if allowed to remain, could be mistaken for the real architecture of English and could prevent us from ever seeing it.

The Effects of Over-simplification

29   Over-simplified 'rules' may seem to help for a time, but they can produce the following effects:

(*a*) Usage is often distorted to support them. The teacher who places his pen firmly on the desk announcing, '*I am putting my pen on the desk*', in obedience to the rule criticised in **18,** is as guilty as the old-fashioned pedagogue who expected his class to translate artificial sentences like *This is the pen of my aunt*; while an utterance like *You are saying that you are putting your pen on the desk* (which I found quoted in a list of 'structures' to be taught in schools) is stylistically horrible.

(*b*) Hours are wasted not only on lessons teaching half-truths as if they were the whole truth, but also on doing exercises which require the student to choose between two constructions, both of which can be perfectly acceptable, though one of the two is falsely supposed to be 'wrong'. An instance of this is the exercise based on the 'rule' that *some* is used only with verbs in the affirmative, *any* only with the negative and interrogative. Expressions like *Would you like some more tea?* and *Any child could tell you that*, both perfectly good English, would be therefore considered 'incorrect'.

(*c*) Over-simplified rules will often remain firmly embedded in the learner's mind. A teacher I knew, whose mother-tongue had no exact equivalents of *a* and *the*, had once been instructed as follows: 'Use *a* when a noun is first introduced, and *the* when the same noun occurs again.' He believed that was the whole truth; and could never understand why the famous line from Shakespeare's *Richard III*, '*A horse, a horse, my kingdom for a horse*' should not be '*A horse, the horse, my kingdom for the horse.*'

(*d*) Above all, an inadequate basic rule will sooner or later have to be modified by a series of sub-rules and exceptions which may cause far more trouble in the end than a basic rule that is more accurate though less temptingly teachable.

CHAPTER 2

Approach to the Problems: Primary Distinctions

Rules and Exceptions

30 The first thing I would ask of my readers is that they accept the weakness of any rule if educated usage does not support it. Though English speakers may sometimes be faced with a choice between one form and another, what they actually say and in what circumstances they say it are matters of fact, and a general statement about usage is incorrect if it is contradicted by the facts of generally accepted usage itself. It is not good enough to pretend that all usage which fails to fit the rules we believe in is exceptional.

31 We should therefore consider the difference between (*a*) irregularities in a system and (*b*) exceptions to a so-called rule. By the logic of Graeco-Latin grammar, which determined the thinking of teachers for centuries, every situation in language had its Rule and every Rule its Exceptions. Now we can establish a rule about *some* parts of the 'solid core' of English grammar, e.g. the plural of nouns, and we can note a number of irregularities in the system. We can call them 'exceptions to the rule' if we like: thus *cow*, *cows*, *goat*, *goats* but *sheep*, *sheep*. It is tempting to do this with the whole of the grammar and assume that there will be exceptions to any rule we formulate. This assumption is dangerous. Though we may say *cow*, *cows* but *sheep*, *sheep*, we cannot allow exceptions to the 'rule' that English-speakers make a mental distinction between one unit and more than one, whatever the name of that unit may be. If we believe that exceptions are inevitable, we can always make that an excuse when our 'rules' fail to work.

Word Order

32 The fact that words are put together in patterns and in a certain order is very important in English grammar. For example, no alternative order is normally possible for the words in the following two sentences:

[1]   Harry has done that job very well.

[2]   That big black American car with the four men in it was stopped by the police.

However, it is not those particular words but what we call the 'elements' of sentence structure (e.g. subject, verb, object etc.) that must go in that order, thus:

[1]   Subject (*Harry*) + verb (*has done*) + object (*that job*) + adjunct, which is here an adverbial of manner (*very well*).

[2]   Determiner (*That*) + adjective referring to size (*big*) + adjective referring to colour (*black*) + adjective referring to origin (*American*) + head-word in a noun phrase (*car*) + prepositional phrase modifying the head-word (*with the four men in it*) + verb (*was stopped*) + prepositional phrase referring to the agent when the verb is passive (*by the police*).

33   Now consider the following:

[3]   Please show me how this works.

[4]   The concert was ⎰ a success
⎱ very good
in the open air
yesterday

In example [3], only a limited set of verbs could replace *show* (e.g. *tell* could, but not *say*, or *explain*). In [4], what follows *was* is an obligatory element: the sentence would be incomplete without it; it can be either a noun (*success*), adjective phrase (*very good*), adverbial of place (*in the open air*) or adverbial of time (*yesterday*)— and because of the tense of *was* it must be an adverbial of past time. Learning to construct sentences on such models is an essential process in mastering 'solid core' grammar, though the analysis is something that can be done at a later stage, if at all.

34   Words also go together in what we call collocations. For example, we try to *do good*, we *make a discovery*, we *pay attention* to somebody or something but *draw someone's attention* to it. We can only learn these collocations through use of the language or by finding suitable examples in a good modern dictionary.

Essential Factors, and Incidental Ones

35 In example [4], paragraph 33, we could not replace *was* by *has been* because of a 'solid core' rule which tells us that we must have the Simple Past and not the Present Perfect, in association with an adverb of past time. But while this association between the Simple Past and a past time adverbial is an important factor, it is not the deciding one in our use of that tense. If I lose my watch and find it again a few days later, I can quite correctly say, *Oh, I found my watch*, without using any past time adverbial. Adverbials undoubtedly play a part in tense usage, but they are usually incidental factors, not essential ones. When I put on a rain-coat, I usually take my umbrella too. When I wear an overcoat, I feel in my pocket for gloves. As a habit (and language is very much a matter of habit), I associate rain-coat with umbrella, and overcoat with gloves. Thus I often put on my rain-coat and pick up my umbrella automatically. But is it not possible that I perform both actions primarily because I know it is raining? Similarly, I may use the Simple Past, e.g. *I found*, in automatic association with an adverb like *yesterday* or *a moment ago*; but is it not possible that I use both expressions primarily because my attention is focused, in both instances, on a specific point in past time detached from the present?

36 We can also say *I've found my watch. Here it is*; and we can argue that the fact that I now have my watch and can show it to you is my reason for using the Present Perfect. But this present evidence—though, again, it is a very important factor— is still only an incidental one, since *I found my watch. Here it is* is equally acceptable.

37 Thus we can say:

[5] I've found my watch. Here it is.
[6] I found my watch. Here it is.
[7] I found my watch yesterday.
[8] *But not* *I've found my watch yesterday.

Present evidence is only an incidental factor in the use of the Present Perfect in [5], since [6] is acceptable also; and because [6] is acceptable, the co-occurrence of *yesterday* is not the essential justification for the Simple Past in [7]. We must therefore look elsewhere (Chapter 5) for the essential deciding factors in our choice of the Simple Past and of the Present Perfect.

38 Nevertheless, it is a good idea in teaching the Simple Past to associate it at first with an adverbial of past time, especially a phrase ending in *ago*, since *ago* means 'back from now'. Later, it can be made clear that such an association, though always possible, is not indispensable. It may also be a good idea to introduce the contrast between the Simple Present and the Present Progressive with the help of adverbials, thus

[9]   We're speaking English *now*.

[10]   We *always* speak our own language at home.

But it would be wrong to leave pupils with a firm impression that the progressive is used because of association with *now*, while the Simple Present is used because of *always*. It would be just as correct to say

[11]   You're *always* writing. Don't you ever read a book?

[12]   I used to write my letters by hand. *Now* I type them.

Indeed, *always*, or a synonym for it, is necessary in [11] if the meaning is 'You never stop writing.' By firmly linking *now* with the progressive and *always* with the Simple Present, we may be preventing our pupils from ever seeing the real distinction in meaning between the two forms.

Distinctions of Thought

39   Since we are concerned in these problems with distinctions of thought, we should look for the essential factors both in the distinctions which all human beings find it necessary to make, and in those that are characteristic of the English-speaking people. Universal distinctions, e.g. between male and female, between one and more than one, will be obvious to the student. (None the less, the student may confuse *he* and *she* for purely phonological reasons; and he may make errors in concord, e.g. putting a singular subject with plural verb, through careless application of the 'solid core' rules.) Other distinctions common to many languages, e.g. between completed and uncompleted activity, or between the act performed once and the frequent repetition of it, will be found in English, but indicated in a particular way which the student may not appreciate. Still other distinctions may be quite unfamiliar to him and he may not at first see that they exist.

40   A language cannot help reflecting the ways of behaviour and thought of the people who speak it as their mother-tongue. English has developed through the centuries in the daily life of people whose instincts—or whose climate, or whatever it may be—impel them to physical action. They think in physical, rather than in abstract, logical or mystical terms. They are matter-of-fact. They like to get on with the job, to get things done, to get results. English-speakers reading this paragraph will want to know where it is all leading to. They are concerned with action, movement, direction, mathematically definite relationships in space. To them, there is an important difference between activity and achievement; still more between the word and the deed. They distinguish sharply between the idea and the reality, the general and the particular, the limitless and the strictly confined, the unspecified and the specific, the symbol and the thing it represents. To questions of fact, they want a straight answer; yes or no. They say, 'You know the answer, you remember it, forget it, like it—or you don't.' On the other hand, they are prepared to concede that the answer may depend entirely on one's point of view, on what exactly one has in mind, on where one wants to put the emphasis. Highly individualistic in a close-knit community, they distinguish between the person and people as a whole, between each one and everybody, between the unit and the mass. They see no harm in a man *saying* what he likes: it is what he *tells* others that may have serious social consequences.

41   That is the sort of attitude I see reflected in English grammar and the sort of criterion I shall be using in this book. One of the basic characteristics of that attitude is faith in the unalterable nature of fact. My first word of advice to those who want to understand English grammar is therefore: prefer the facts of authentic and acceptable usage to the grammarian's rules. The grammarian can provide the student with rules which will prepare him for some of the facts he will meet, but not for all of them. There is no way of anticipating idiomatic conventions such as *go to school* side by side with *go to the theatre*, or *fail to do something* with *succeed in doing it*. However, I hope that by the time he has finished this book the reader will be able to recognise and form in his own mind the distinctions which have become stereotyped in such idiomatic phrases and which in the living language are constantly at work.

Grammar as a System of Pairs: Marked and Unmarked Members

42   We generally have to choose one or the other of a *pair*. One member of a pair may stand in contrast to the other; or each may stand in contrast, in its own way, to some element outside the pair. (Cp. R. W. Zandvoort, *Handbook of English Grammar* (Longman, 1975) '. . . we have in English the formal opposition illustrated by such pairs as *boy–boys*, and *boy–boy's*; among the personal pronouns we have the pair *I–we*, and *I–me*, and the set of three *he–she–it*. It is around such oppositions that the grammatical system of the language is to a large extent built up.') As we shall be continually referring to contrast in this book, let us use the symbol *v* instead of 'in contrast to'. Thus we may have *every v each*; *all v every*; *all v each*; *a v the*; *no article v a*; *no article v the*; and many others.

43　One member of a pair can be *marked* in some way; the other *unmarked* in that way; or both may be marked, each standing in contrast in a different way with something unmarked. To appreciate the principle involved here, notice the marked and unmarked members in the following pairs of words:

Unmarked		Marked
horse	v	mare
duck	v	drake
school	v	kindergarten

Ordinarily we speak of a *horse* whether the animal is male or female. In saying *mare* we are specially concerned with the fact that the animal is a female of the species. In other words, we use the marked form when we wish to make a particular distinction, the unmarked form when that distinction is not felt to be necessary. Notice that we can say *horse* even though we know the animal is female: in that case, we do not feel the distinction worth making, or it is not there that we wish to place the emphasis. Notice, also, that we *must* say *horse* when we wish to indicate that the creature is male, not female. (*Horse v stallion* forms a less common pair. In *stallion v mare* both members are marked in contrast to *horse*.) We can summarise the matter thus:

	Unmarked	Marked
1	horse (sex of no concern; either sex)	mare (female in contrast to male)
2	horse (male in contrast to female)	

I shall call the first *horse* the *weak* unmarked form; the second *horse*, *strong*. With *duck* and *drake* the roles are reversed: the female happens to be unmarked, the male is the marked member. With *school* and *kindergarten* we have:

1	school (for children of all ages)	kindergarten (for small children only, not older)

2 school (for older children,
above kindergarten age)

44 The difference between the marked and the unmarked member
of a pair is the particular distinction made on the marked member
but not on the unmarked; for example, it is the distinction we wish
to make when we use *mare* instead of *horse*, *drake* instead of *duck*,
kindergarten instead of *school*. If you like, we might say that *horse*,
duck and *school* are the norms, the other words are variants. What
particular distinction do we wish to make when we use *mare* instead
of horse, *drake* instead of *duck*? Is it a question of size? It might be,
incidentally. Is it a question of colour? Again, it might be. But it is
of course primarily one of sex. A distinctive feature of a kindergarten might be the smallness of the classroom furniture; but it is
primarily the fact that it is designed for children of a certain age.

45 The contrast between unmarked and marked applies to both
lexis (i.e. the words we use, *horse* or *mare*) and to grammar. I would
regard the Simple Present as unmarked and the Present Progressive
as marked: that is to say, the former is the norm, while the latter
is used when we wish to make some special emphasis. As with *horse
v mare*, *duck v drake*, *school v kindergarten*, there may be incidental
differences between members of a grammatical pair, and essential
ones. For example, the fact that *in* is used with reference to a capital
city while *at* is used with a place with fewer inhabitants is not the
essential distinction in the contrast *in v at*. You will not find CAPITAL
CITY *v* VILLAGE among the primary distinctions listed in paragraph
46.

Primary Distinctions

46   A. Aspects of things that we refer to by nouns

1   CONCRETE *v* ABSTRACT
The distinction between a common noun, e.g. *table*, referring to
something having physical substance, and an abstract noun, e.g.
kindness, is still often taught in the earliest lessons in English
grammar. However, far more important is the difference between
unit nouns and mass nouns (see 5 below). What the student has to
learn about abstract nouns is really as follows:

(*a*) Their morphology, i.e. how they are formed, so that he can
easily change e.g. *Thank you for being kind* to *Thank you for your
kindness.*

(*b*) With what other words they collocate (see **34**). Thus: *We discovered something interesting* can be re-phrased *We made an interesting discovery.* There is a distinction between concrete and abstract which appears in the following examples:

[13]   We arrived at the right station.
[14]   We arrived at the right conclusion.

A passive transformation of [14] is quite acceptable, *The right conclusion was arrived at*, but is unlikely to occur with [13].

2   INANIMATE *v* ANIMATE

The distinction between animate (i.e. living) things and inanimate is especially important in deciding what words can act as subject or as object of what verbs. Note what kind of nouns can act as subject and object of *delight, enjoy, remember, remind*:

[15]   Hector and his songs delighted the audience.
[16]   The whole audience thoroughly enjoyed his performance.
[17]   The ladies will always remember him and his music.
[18]   Hector and his songs of long ago reminded the old folk of happier days.

Furthermore, the genitive with apostrophe *s* will not normally occur with a noun referring to something inanimate, though it does occur with nouns referring to human beings, human institutions, animals and birds; and the indirect object (see examples in Chapter 7) will always be a noun or pronoun referring to something animate, except in cases like *Please give my car a wash*. We can take our passports to an officer or to an office, but only the 'animate' noun is allowable in the sentence *Take the officer your passport*.

3   HUMAN (AND NEAR-HUMAN) *v* NON-HUMAN

Within the inanimate v animate distinction, there is the question of whether or not something animate is human, or closely associated with human beings, or is completely impersonal. Notice how this affects the use of the interrogative *Who?*, which asks for the identity of a human being (though it could, in families that are very fond of pets, apply to a domestic animal); and of the interrogative *What?*, asking for the identity of something impersonal. It affects relative pronouns, *who* (or *that*) and *whom* being reserved for personal antecedents, and *which* (or *that*) for impersonal ones. *He* and *she* replace only nouns referring to male and female humans or to domestic animals whose sex is known and relevant. *She* is often used by a proud owner, usually male, when referring to a machine or ship (*She's a beauty, isn't she?*), though this odd usage should not be regarded as obligatory: *it* would be a perfectly acceptable alternative. Examples of human/near-human/non-human distinctions are:

[19] Who were those two men who arrived very late last night?

[20] What is that animal with black stripes? It looks like a horse, or a donkey, with pyjamas on.

[21] A. Has Bob taken the dog for a walk?
B. Yes, he took it (*or* him *or* her) out an hour ago.

4 SUBSTANCE *v* OBJECT consisting of that substance

We can have the substance *stone* (*A stone wall is a wall made of stone.*), or an object consisting of that substance (*Wait for me. I've a stone in my shoe.*). We can also have the substances *wood* and *metal*, and separate objects, e.g. *chairs*, made of those substances. There is a similar distinction between *material* (i.e. something that has been made, like *cloth* or *paper*) and a particular object, e.g. *a cloth*, *a paper*, composed of that material.

5 MASS *v* UNIT

We can regard the substance, stone, or the material, cloth, as an undivided mass, and the objects stones, chairs, cloths and papers as units that can be counted. This distinction is very important in modern English grammar, as we shall see (Chapter 3). Abstract nouns, e.g. *kindness*, *education*, tend to be mass nouns; but many can also occur as unit nouns (*You've done me a great kindness. He had a good education.*); and some abstract nouns (e.g. *an idea*, *a scheme*) occur only as unit nouns. With the distinction between mass and unit, goes that between *amount* (of a mass) and *number* (of units).

6 CLASS (of substance or object) *v* MEMBER or example of that class

A cat, in *A cat is a domestic animal*, refers to the whole class of things which we could identify as cats; whereas *a cat*, in *Monty has a cat*, refers to one member only of that class. Similarly, *wood* in *Wood floats in water*, refers to the whole class of a certain substance; whereas *wood*, in *a piece of wood*, refers to one example of it only.

7 GENERAL *v* PARTICULAR

Language and *students* are general in the contexts *Language is a means of communication* and *Students often don't eat enough*. *The language* and *The students* are particular in *He speaks the language well* and *The students are drinking coffee*. But see 8.

8   UNSPECIFIED *v* SPECIFIED

In the last two examples of 7, *The language* and *The students* refer to a particular language and to particular students, but they are not, by themselves, specified. They would be specified in *The language we are now studying* and *The students who ought to be sitting here.*

9   UNLIMITED *v* LIMITED

We can have an unlimited amount or number, as in *Take any of this material, or any of these books that you want,* or a limited amount or number, as in *I hope you will leave some of it, or some of them, for me.* Unlimited choice is implied by *What book would you like?,* while *Which book?* limits the choice to a specified number.

10   WHOLE *v* PART

We can have *all,* i.e. *the whole* of an amount or of a number, or *some,* i.e. part of that amount or number.

11   ONE *v* MORE THAN ONE

This is the well-known difference between singular and plural.

12   TWO *v* MORE THAN TWO

Both, each, either, neither, refer to two units; *all, each, every, any, none* refer to more than two.

B. Aspects of activity that we refer to by verbs

13   GENERAL *v* PARTICULAR (see 7 above)

We refer to the general activity of swimming in *Fish swim in water* but to particular performances of it in *We swim in the river every morning.* The progressive form of the verb is very unlikely to be used when the speaker is referring to the activity in general: it is much more likely to be used with reference to particular performances as in *I know where Dick and Harry are. They're swimming in the lake.*

14   The ACT as a WHOLE *v* the UNCOMPLETED ACTION (see 10 above)

The act as a whole is emphasised in *I've read your book*; the uncompleted action in *I've been reading it.*

15   The ACTION ITSELF *v* the ACTION FINISHED

Focus is on the action itself in *Drink,* as in *Drink a pint of milk a day*; in the action finished in *drink up,* in *You haven't finished your medicine—drink it up.*

16 The ACTION *v* the RESULT ACHIEVED
Focus is on the action in *do*, e.g. *What are you doing? Are you busy?*
It is on the result in *make*, as in *I'm making some book-shelves.*

17 An EVENT *v* a STATE OF AFFAIRS
The verb refers to an event occurring at a point in time, in *We moved to London in 1968*, but to a state of affairs lasting throughout a period of time in *We have lived here for eight years.* Notice how this affects the tense associated with *since*:

[22] Since we moved here (*since that event*), we've made many new friends.

[23] Since we've lived here (*while that state of affairs has continued*), many of our old friends have come to see us.

18 POINT-OF-TIME ACTION *v* ACTIVITY HAVING DURATION
In *I've shut the door*, *shut* refers to point-of-time action: while *He's shutting* refers to a series of acts, or to activity having duration, in

[24] It's time to go. The caretaker is shutting all the doors.

The progressive form of the verb is unlikely to occur in natural English with reference to a single point-of-time act: it is much more likely with activity having duration.

19 DYNAMIC *v* NON-DYNAMIC (or STATIVE)
Most verbs refer to 'dynamic activity' over which we have control and which can therefore be performed deliberately and purposefully: e.g. *look, listen, walk, run.* But certain verbs, called 'stative', do not refer to purposeful activity: they express a relationship, as in the case of *be* and *have*, or sensory or mental states, as in the case of *see, hear, know, understand.* 'Dynamic' verbs can easily occur in the progressive, with adverbs of manner (e.g. *carefully*) and with expressions of purpose; whereas 'stative' verbs will normally not occur under those conditions. Thus:

[25] I was looking at the signature carefully (*adverb of manner*) to make sure it was mine (*purpose*).

but not **I was seeing it carefully to make sure* etc.

20 MOVEMENT FROM ONE PLACE TO ANOTHER *v* NO SUCH MOVEMENT
Go, come, drive, fly all imply movement from place to place and are used with prepositions of movement (*to, into* etc.: see Chapter 9). *Be, stay, live, work* do not imply such movement and occur with prepositions of position (*at, in,* etc.).

21   FREEDOM TO ACT *v* LACK OF FREEDOM

The modals, *will, shall, would, should, can, could, may, might, must* and *ought* will be considered (in Chapter 6) as expressing varying degrees of freedom to act, from absolute freedom to complete lack of it. (They will also be considered as expressing various degrees of certainty on the part of the speaker with regard to the statement he is making.)

C. Aspects of time

22   UNLIMITED *v* LIMITED (see 9)

Unlimited time is expressed by the Present Time only; limited time by Present, Past or Future.

23   PRESENT TIME *v* TIME NO LONGER, or NOT YET PRESENT

All time is considered as present until we give some indication (e.g. *yesterday, tomorrow*) that we have marked off part of it as non-present.

24   POINT-OF-TIME *v* PERIOD (see 17)

In *I had been waiting since the accident happened, that is to say for half an hour. I waited till the ambulance arrived,* the accident happened at one point of time, the ambulance arrived at another; *since* marks the point at which a period of time began, *till* marks the point at which a period ended; *for* signals the length of a period.

25   PERMANENT *v* TEMPORARY

Adjectives that can be used attributively (e.g. *a strong, healthy man*) tend to refer to a permanent condition, while those that occur only predicatively (*The baby is awake*) tend to refer to a temporary state of affairs.

D. Aspects of space

26   NO, or UNSPECIFIED, DIMENSION *v* ONE, TWO or THREE DIMENSIONS

Unspecified dimension, or no dimension, is associated with *at*, e.g. *Wait at the door. Stop at that point*; whereas *on* would be more often associated with one dimension (*on the line*) or two (*on the surface*), and *in* with three (*in a space or area*).

27   MOVEMENT *v* POSITION (see 20)

We can consider movement to a destination, position at that point, movement away from it, and position away from it, thus:

──────────────→	○	going to
	×	being at
←──────────────	○	going away from
×	○	being away from

E. Degree

28   GRADABLE *v* UNGRADABLE

There can be degrees of hardness, softness, goodness, etc., so that we can say *very hard*, (*not*) *hard enough*, *too hard*, *harder*, *hardest*, and so on. But there are no degrees of, say, *unique-ness*, so that **very unique*, **more unique*, etc. are unacceptable. *Hard* is therefore called gradable, *unique* ungradable. A similar distinction can be applied to adverbs—*very carefully*, (*not*) *carefully enough* (gradable) but not **very completely* (ungradable). It can also be applied to verbs; *like* and *appreciate* are gradable, but *see* and *meet* are not; hence the different adverbial in *I like, or appreciate, that very much*, but *I see, or meet, him very often*.

F. Affirmative, negative, interrogative

29   AFFIRMATIVE ASSERTION *v* NEGATION or DOUBT

Some, *already* and *too* are normally associated with affirmative statements and with questions that expect or imply an affirmative answer. *Any*, *yet* and *either* are normally associated with negatives or with questions that seem prepared for either a negative or affirmative reply. Thus:

[26]   A. I've found some mistakes in this book already.
      B. I've found some, too. Have you found some (*or* any)?
      C. I haven't found any yet.
      D. I haven't found any either.

G. Apposition and relative clauses

30   RESTRICTIVE *v* NON-RESTRICTIVE

Consider the following examples:

[27]   Everything comes to the man who waits.
[28]   Nothing could annoy my Uncle Tom, who was the most patient man alive.
[29]   I know your friend Tom Jackson very well.
[30]   Christopher Columbus, the discoverer of America, died in 1506.

In [27], the relative clause, *who waits*, is restrictive or defining: it answers the question *What man?* In [28], the relative clause, *who was* etc., is non-restrictive; it does not answer the question *Which Uncle Tom?*, but supplies additional information about him. Similarly, in [29], *Tom Jackson* is in restrictive apposition to *your friend*: it tells us which of your friends; in [30], *the discoverer of America* is in non-restrictive apposition to Christopher Columbus. The significance of this is as follows: *that* could replace *who* in [27], but not in [28]; and commas, with a break in intonation, are obligatory in [28] and [30], but would not occur in [27] and [29].

H. Matters of fact

31   FACT *v* NON-FACT
Were refers to fact in *You were here yesterday*, but to non-fact in *I wish you were here today* (*but you're not*).

47   We must also take into account:

(*a*) What exactly the speaker has to mind at the time of speaking. The important thing is not what the object to which he refers is in reality, but what he imagines it to be at the time. '*At a place*' is 'right' if the speaker imagines that place as a point on the map. '*In it*' is 'right' if he sees it as a space-area. We can say *the committee thinks* if we have in mind *a body* of people, or *the committee think* if we have in mind a body of *individual persons*. Both are acceptable, so long as the speaker does not change his point of view erratically. He may say *The committee have finished their work*, but not put *has* with *their*, or *have* with *its*. Nevertheless, in unscripted speech even good speakers change their mental image in the middle of a sentence; but it is safer to avoid this in writing.

(*b*) The speaker's point of view; and particularly the point in space or in time which is of primary concern to the speaker at the moment he speaks. The importance of the speaker's point of view is obvious in *here* and *there*, *this* and *that*. It will be found to play a considerable part in tense usage. It affects the use of *come* and *go*, *bring* and *take*, *up* and *down*. *Come* indicates movement in the same direction as the speaker, or towards his 'point of view' or 'point of primary concern', which might be either where he is or where the person he is addressing happens to be; *go*, in any other direction. *Bring* (*something*) corresponds more or less to *come with* (*it*); *take* (*it*), more or less to *go with* (*it*). *Up* indicates direction not only towards a higher physical level but also towards a place to which the speaker attaches greater importance, though within a certain area, e.g. a country; *down,* not only towards a lower level but also a place of lesser importance; although these considerations may be outweighed by others, such as *up north* and *down south.*

How the Right Choice is Made

48   The 'right choice' of construction might therefore be said to result from an association between (*a*) the particular 'aspect' that the speaker has in mind and wishes to emphasise, and (*b*) the construction he selects. That association must be acceptable to educated native speakers of the language. It may have to be adjusted according to the way in which individual words happen to be treated. For example, *an iron* is a household implement, originally made of the substance *iron*; but *a wood* usually signifies a group of trees. Moreover, the association must be the essential one. For instance, the distinction between permanent and temporary may help us to see why we can say *My aunt is unwell* but cannot say **My unwell aunt.* I might have that same distinction in mind when I say *My aunt is living in a furnished apartment, temporarily*; but that is not the essential distinction between *is living* and *lives.* We could not use the temporary/permanent contrast to justify *She's being unwell* (which might suggest that she is in the uncompleted act of being sea-sick).

Fixed Expressions and Freedom of Choice

49   There are a great many fixed expressions in which the speaker finds the right correlation readymade. In natural speech they are produced automatically. Take for example the expressions *to school* and *at school* in the contexts *In most countries all children now have to go to school* and *They stay at school until they are fourteen or fifteen.* In both cases we refer to the concept *school* in general, and use no article; we do not wish to specify the institution—in fact, our emphasis is on something else, namely the education given at school. In the first case we are interested in *movement, going (to)*; in the second, with *position, dimension unspecified.* Now, are *to the school, at the school, in school* or *in the school* 'correct'? Yes, all are if they correspond with what we mean; in other words, if we have good reason for using those marked forms, and if they reflect, in a socially acceptable way, some special distinction that we wish to make. *To the school* (movement) and *at the school* (position) might be described as marked members of the pairs *to school v to the school* and *at school v at the school*, where we use the signal *the* to show that we are referring not to school in the abstract but to one identifiable school as distinct from another or from others or as distinct from something else. Thus:

[31]   In some countries parents are obliged to send their children to the school nearest their home.

[32]   I know Dr Berry—he taught at the school I used to go to.

Then we have the pair *at school v in school* in which we use the marked member, *in school*, to stress the idea of being in *a space* without specifying the institution; e.g.

[33]   You must stay in school till the bus comes to fetch you— it's far too wet to go out.

An example of *in the school* would be

[34]   'Every room in the school' (*the Headmaster complained, referring specifically to his own school*) 'is overcrowded.'

50   Word-groups like *at school* and *in school* tend to form part of larger groups and to become associated with certain situations. Thus *stay at school* is customarily used to mean *stay at this place called school* or *continue to be a school pupil*, while *stay in school* is used to mean *remain inside the building*. A perfect command of English may therefore depend on the speaker's knowing what words and word-groups are commonly used in combination with one another and precisely in what social situation each is employed. But if that were invariably true the learner's task would be endless and English would not be free—as it is, to a remarkable extent—to adapt itself to new situations. The main argument of this book is that the kind of distinctions described in **46** and discernible in stereotyped expressions like *stay at school* and *stay in school* are those that determine free and original usage.

CHAPTER 3

The Articles

51 All English sentences have two main components—the Noun Phrase, of which a noun is the nucleus, and the Verb Phrase. The articles—*a, the* or zero (the concept of zero, which here refers to the absence of an article, is a very old one in the study of grammar, and is commonly used by modern grammarians)—are an important part of the noun phrase. They belong to a class of word now called 'determiners'. A determiner very often accompanies and precedes a common noun, for this reason: a common noun is the name of a class of thing (e.g. *cat* in **46A** 6); and with such a common noun we usually have to indicate which member or members of the class, or what quantity of it, we have in mind. Determiners therefore either identify and are identifiers (answering the question *Which?*), or quantify and are quantifiers (answering the question *How much?* or *How many?*). The articles identify, definitely or indefinitely.

52 The problems with the articles are to decide whether to use (*a*) zero or *a*, (*b*) zero or *the*, (*c*) *a* or *the*. There is also the difficulty of knowing when words should be, or are customarily, put into the plural. So we must also decide whether to use the singular or the plural form.

53 The primary distinctions that apply to those four problems are: mass v unit; general v particular; unspecified v specific; substance v object consisting of such substance; one v more than one.

54 The distinction between mass and unit is of prime importance in the use of the articles. There are nouns that are invariably mass nouns, e.g. *bread, music, poetry*; others that are invariably unit nouns, e.g. *loaf, book, poem*; others that can be used either as mass nouns or as unit nouns. Those used as mass nouns are not preceded by *a*, nor used in the plural. Those used as unit nouns can have *a* and a plural. Generally speaking, mass nouns include the nouns of solid substances and materials (*stone, wood, cloth, paper*); of liquids and gases (*water, oil, air, smoke*) and of languages (*English, French*). Most abstract nouns are normally mass nouns, e.g. *advice, beauty, behaviour, fun, harm, information, knowledge, leisure, progress.* Certain words, whose equivalent in other languages would occur in the plural, are singular mass nouns in English, e.g. *furniture, luggage, news.* Unit nouns include the names of persons, animals, plants (*man, horse, rose*); objects having a distinct shape (*ball, hammer, house, tube*); units of measurement (*hour, kilometre*); and a few abstractions (*idea, nuisance, scheme*).

55   The terms 'countable' (or 'count') and 'uncountable' are often used instead of mass and unit. I have avoided them in this book, having found that they often lead to confused thinking. Consider the statement 'Egg is countable.' The things we call eggs are of course countable. The single word *egg* is not countable beyond one. Egg, the substance, is uncountable, as in the following dialogue:

> Grandmother   *I know what you had for breakfast this morning.*
> Grandchild   *What did I have then?*
> Grandmother   *Egg.*
> Grandchild   *How do you know?*
> Grandmother   *Because you have egg on your chin.*
> Grandchild   *Well, you're wrong. I had egg yesterday.*

On the other hand, *money* is called an uncountable, although the counting of money must be one of the commonest of human activities.[1]

The Noun Unmarked—Without Any Article

56   A set of pictures designed for teaching reading to native English-speaking children contained one like this:

Apple

Fig. 2

[1] I am indebted to Dr D. P. L. Dry for the story of the student who justified 'People was everywhere' on the grounds that the people were uncountable!

The children were expected to copy that picture, writing 'apple' at the bottom: not 'an apple' or 'the apple', but simply 'apple'. The designer of the picture had assumed that the need for the special distinction made by *a, an* or *the* had not yet arisen. The child's mind was not to be confused by the possibility of there being other apples, or other things from which the object he was drawing had to be distinguished. The thing he was drawing filled the picture.

57 Take another example. According to an ancient story, before men began to build the Tower of Babel so that they could climb up to Heaven, they spoke one tongue. The idea of other languages had never occurred to them. In such a situation we would say, 'Men used language to speak with one another,' just as we can still say, 'Man is superior to the animals in that he uses language to convey his thoughts.' Let us represent 'language' thus:

Language

Fig. 3

The Noun Marked to Indicate an Unspecified Number of Units

58 Later in the set of pictures mentioned in **56,** this illustration was provided:

Apples

Fig. 4

The picture contained, as it happened, seven apples. But the actual number was not important. The purpose of the exercise was simply to present children with a picture filled with apples, to let them copy it and write 'apples' at the bottom.

59   The story of Babel goes on to tell us that as a punishment for their trying to climb up to Heaven men were made to speak different languages. Figure 3 then becomes:

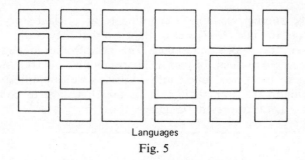

Languages

Fig. 5

60   A film or television camera could move away from Fig. 2 to produce Fig. 4—telescopically as it were. It could take a close-up of Fig. 3 to produce Fig. 5—microscopically. Note that if Fig. 3 represented a mass of water, the camera moving towards it would show a smaller area of water; away from it, a larger area; but it would not show water as a group of units.

61   In Fig. 2 and Fig. 3 we have an unmarked form; we are concerned with an undivided whole; the concept in general; an example of the concept not distinguished from other examples or from different concepts; the concept that fills the picture. In Fig. 4 and Fig. 5 we are using a marked form to show that we are particularly concerned with the two concepts in terms of units—with apples and languages in general. The choice of *apple v apples* or *language v languages* is therefore a matter of concept in general v units in general.

The Noun Marked to Indicate One, Unspecified Example

62   Select any one of the units in Fig. 4 or Fig. 5. You now have one complete example of the concept—an apple or a language—an example that is a separate, complete unit by itself. 'An apple' or 'a language' could be written under each one of the units in Fig. 4 and Fig. 5. We could express *apple v an apple* as *concept in general v one complete, independent but unspecified example of it. An* (before a vowel sound) and *a* (before a consonant sound) might be considered as unemphasised forms of *one*. In the pair *a* (or *an*) v *one*, we use the marked form *one* to stress the idea of 'one and not more than one', or 'one and not another', as in

[1]   There's only one apple left

or

[2]   One man's meat is another man's poison.

We also use *one* as a substitute for *a* + noun, as in

[3]   A. Will you have an apple?
      B. Thank you, I have one. (*i.e. I have an apple*).

Note also the use of *one*, not *a*, in a sentence like

[4]   One day, as we were sitting quietly in the garden, an elephant walked in.

63   Note that *an apple* is one of all the things called by that name, i.e. one of a class. In that formula, *one of a class*, the emphasis can fall on *class* or on the quantity, *one*. Notice how this difference of emphasis operates in the following table:

Singular	*Plural*	*Emphasis on*
This is an apple	These are apples	Class
I'd like an apple	I'd like some apples	Quantity + class

64   Note also that *a language* is an independent whole; it is not merely a fragment or sample. A fragment or sample of language would be *language* with the zero article, as in *This sentence contains language*. There, I am using *language* to mean, not *language in general*, but one sample of it, although the same form is used for both. Likewise, a fragment of apple is simply *apple*, just as a trace of egg is simply *egg* (**55**). If we are concerned with the size of the sample, we can use *some*, as in:

	Emphasis on
This is water	Class
May I have some water?	Quantity + class

65   *A* is by tradition called 'the indefinite article'. It can in fact point to both a completely indefinite unit (*I want a pencil—any one will do*) or a more definite one (*A man called to see you while you were out. Here's his card*). In any case, we may call it an indefinite identifier.

The Plural of 'An Apple', 'A Language'

66 Next, pick out more than one of the units in Fig. 4 and Fig. 5, and you have *apples* and *languages*. This is the same form as for **58** and **59**, and explains why the same word *languages* could be translated into French in two ways, namely *les langues* (languages in general), *des langues* (more than one language). To stress the quantity 'more than one', we can use one of the quantifiers that will be discussed in the next chapter, e.g. *some, a few, a lot of*. So the difference in emphasis mentioned in **63** is clearly made in the plural. There is emphasis on quantity in *some eggs* in

[5]   A. Is there anything else you want, madam?
     B. Yes. I'd like some eggs please,

but emphasis on the class of thing in

[6]   Would you like eggs for breakfast, or something else?

The Noun Marked with 'The'

67 Select one of the units from Fig. 4 again. Which one have you chosen, *this* one or *that* one? Let us put a mark round the one you have chosen. We are now concerned with one specified unit and no other. Now we have *the apple*. Which apple? The one we have marked, as distinct from all the rest.

This is the apple

Fig. 6

68 Once the unit has been identified, *the* serves as a weak form for *this* or *that* and makes it unnecessary for those words to be repeated. Note that *this* and *that*, and other definite identifiers such as *these*, *those*, *my*, *your*, *his*, *her*, *our*, *their* and a name with apostrophe *s*, e.g. *Shakespeare's*, are felt to be sufficient by themselves to identify the thing we are talking about. They are not accompanied by *the*, so that **the Shakespeare's theatre* is unacceptable. On the other hand, *the* is *not* sufficient by itself to identify the unit. It functions as *a signal of specification*—a signal by which the speaker conveys the message 'You know, or will know, the thing I mean.' The actual specification is provided by something else: see **103**. In any case, if I say *Take the apple* I am assuming you know which one I mean. Notice also that while *this* and *that* can be used as pronouns, *the* cannot be. I can say *Take this* (*one*) or *that* (*one*) or *Take it*, but not **Take the*.

69 Now if all the units in Fig. 6 except the one marked were fruit other than apples, then in saying *Take the apple* I would be specifying that object called an apple as distinct from objects not belonging to that class. And if all the objects in Fig. 6 were taken away except the one marked, so that there was only one object in front of us, namely an apple, then in saying *Take the apple*, I would obviously be specifying that object.

70 The functions of *the* might be demonstrated as follows:

X

This is an X. (Note there is only one.)

(*a*) X [X] or X X [X] X
The same X, marked to distinguish it from
another X or from other X's.

(*b*) Y [X] Z or Y Z [X] Y Z
The X, marked to distinguish it from a Y or
a Z, or from Y's or Z's.

(*c*)   [X]
the X—it is perfectly clear which one I mean.

---

71 In **70** (*a*), the emphasis is on *that member of a class* as distinct from others of the same class; and here the function of *the* is to signal specification within a class. In **70** (*b*) the emphasis is on *that class* as distinct from another class or from other classes. In **70** (*c*), the emphasis is on *that member*; and here the function is to specify an object which, *in the context*, stands as the solitary example of its kind.

72 'The solitary example present of its kind' can bear a mark of distinction in a double sense: it is distinguished from other things by its solitariness, and it can acquire distinction in the sense of 'prestige'. This is noticeable in *the President*, *the Headmaster*, *the Rector*, *the MacDonald* (the chief of the MacDonald Clan), *the kilt* (that special kind of garment, regarded by the Scots with pride).

73 The three categories in **70** are marked by differences of stress, noticeable when the noun is preceded by an adjective; thus:

(*a*) *Which will you have, the 'red apple or the 'green one?* (Stress on the adjectives, *red* and *green*.)

(*b*) *The young 'student often thinks he knows more than the experienced 'teacher.* (Stress on the nouns.)

(*c*) *The dis'tinguished 'president of our country. The 'blue 'sea.* (Stress on both adjectives and nouns, more or less equally.)

74 There is another way of looking at **70** (*c*). If we consider the separate parts of what is in the square in **70**, we see that a certain point in the pattern is picked out from the rest. In other words, some object, some point in space, is specially marked. Imagine that the square contains a plan of your room or of your house, or a map of the district you live in; and that X represents a specified object in the room, or part of your house, or place in the town. In referring to that object or whatever it may be, you and the person you are addressing may know that other objects of the same class exist, but you and he know perfectly well which one you have in mind. In English, we are constantly referring to definite, marked objects and places on the map of our domestic, social and personal experience. Thus, on the plan of my room I indicate *the door*, *the floor*, *the ceiling*; of my house, *the kitchen*, *the dining-room*, *the stairs*, *the bathroom*; of the ground where my house stands, *the garden*, *the lawn*; of the surroundings, *the road*, *the pavement*; of the district I live in, *the post-office*, *the grocer's*, *the bank*, *the railway station*, *the church*, *the school*, *the theatre*, *the market*; beyond, *the country*, *the sea*, *the sky*. I do not give these objects an exclusive name, such as *London*; I use a name that can be applied to other objects of the same kind.

75 Examples of **70**:

(*a*)   [7] Here are two apples: you may have the 'bigger one.

       [8] Here are three: we'll cut the 'biggest in half.

(*b*)   [9] Which is heavier, this 'egg or this 'stone? The 'stone.

    [10] The 'lion (*an imaginary representative of a class, as distinct from animals of other classes*) is the king of beasts.

[11] The (*imaginary*) 'student, as distinct from the (*imaginary*) 'teacher.

(*c*) [12] The table—*the one I am writing at.*

[13] The ceiling—*the ceiling of this room.*

[14] The President (*of our country*) will arrive at half past two.

[15] The student (*the imaginary class-representative we keep talking about*) sometimes does not know more than the teacher.

[16] The sun (*the sun we all know*) sets in the west.

76 Whichever way one looks at it, therefore, *a v the* is a question of *unspecified unit v unit specified in the context, or assumed by the speaker to be identifiable by the hearer.*

77 Similarly *the language* would be a specified, complete example of language, e.g. *the English language*. However, it could also refer to a specified fragment or sample (see **64**); thus *I hope the language I am using now is not too obscure* or *The egg on the child's chin* (**55**) *had come from the breakfast he had eaten the day before.*

'The' with the Plural Form of the Noun

78 *The apples, the languages,* can then be explained as specific units, corresponding to *these* or *those apples,* etc. The pronoun in the plural would be *Take these, or those. Take the ones you have chosen. Take them.* There would be the same change of emphasis as in **70**. Thus, an example of **70** (*a*) in the plural would be

[17] These are not the apples I ordered;

of **70** (*b*)

[18] Divide the sheep from the goats;

of **70** (*c*)

[19] The stars are very bright tonight.

79 We do not, however, use the plural form to refer to specified fragments of a mass (cp. **77**), so that *apples* or *languages* do not mean 'pieces of apples' or 'samples of language'. We would have to refer to specified fragments by such expressions as *pieces of apple, traces of egg, pieces of language* or *drops of water. Drops of water* will be discussed further in **93**.

Summary of the Uses of the Articles

80   We can now make up a set of six 'aspects' for the uses of the articles in modern English, thus:

Aspect	Examples		Meaning
1	apple	language	the concept in general, the mass or sample of a mass; the unmarked form
2	apples	languages	the concept in general, but seen as a complete collection of units
3	an apple	a language	one, complete, unspecified unit chosen from the whole collection
4	apples	languages	more than one of those units—but not the whole lot
5	the apple	the language	one example, either a complete unit or a sample, assumed by the speaker to be identifiable by the hearer
6	the apples	the languages	more than one identifiable unit (but not more than one identifiable sample)

81   Potentially, every noun in English could be considered from each of those six points of view. In practice, because of the nature of the things we talk about, or because of the native English-speaker's conception of them, or for historical reasons, or simply because of fashion, some nouns fill all six of those positions more easily and frequently than others do. *Stone*, the substance from which buildings and statues are made, fills positions 1 and 5; *stone*, the object that one can pick up and throw, fills positions 2, 3, 4, 5 and 6. *Man* can fill all six positions, even the first (*Man is a thinking animal*). The abstract mass noun, *knowledge*, besides filling positions 1 and 5, could fill 3 also (*A knowledge of English is essential*); but *knowledges* is a potential rather than an actual usage: it *could* occur in literature, but ordinary users of English would be wise to leave it to creative writers to experiment with.

82   For ordinary purposes, nouns fall into three groups according to the articles they require:

(i)   *Proper nouns*, e.g. *Shakespeare*, which normally occur in aspect 1 only.

(ii)   *Unit nouns*, e.g. *apple*, which normally occur in all six aspects except the first, thus:

2   Apples grow on trees.
3   This is an apple. Here is an apple.
4   These are apples. Here are some apples.
5   This is the apple mentioned in 3.
6   These are the apples mentioned in 4.

A few unit nouns would normally occur only in aspect 5, e.g. *the sun, the moon, the sea, the sky*, as in **70** (*c*).

(iii)   *Mass nouns*, e.g. *water, music*, which normally occur only in aspects 1 and 5, e.g.

1   Water is heavier than air. This is water, not oil.
5   The water here is excellent.

83   The dividing line between those groups is not always easy to draw. Is *breakfast*, in *Breakfast is at eight*, a unit noun used as a mass noun? The difficulty of drawing a line, as well as the fact that there is a line to be drawn, emerges from the following test:

Apply the question *What is. . .?* to *apple, knowledge, sea* and we shall get *What is an apple? What is knowledge? What is the sea?* With other nouns we could produce either *What is iron?* or *What is an iron?*, *What is language?* or *What is a language?* With regard to *breakfast*, the normal native-English form of the question would be *What is breakfast?*

Articles with Proper Nouns

84   We have already had *the Shakespeare* (in **16**). We could also have *a Shakespeare*, i.e. a man with that kind of genius; and even *Shakespeares*, as in *There are not many Shakespeares in the world* (i.e. not many men like him). *The* is often used with family names, as in *the Barretts*, the family of people named Barrett.

85   Names of countries and other geographical areas begin with *the* when they are composed of unit nouns. *The Union of Soviet Socialist Republics* is an example of **70** (*a*), and tells us *Which union?* *The United States, the British Isles, the Philippine Islands*, are examples of **70** (*a*) in the plural, telling us *Which states?* etc. Columbus, sailing west to reach India, discovered several new Indias instead, and gave us *the Indies*, plural of **70** (*c*). *The Peak*, the name of a mountain, is an example of **70** (*c*) singular.

86   Apart from countries with political boundaries, such as those quoted in **85**, certain geographical features which have to be distinguished one from another also have names beginning with *the*. *The Red Sea* is a specified sea, and so is *the Indian Ocean*. *The Giant Mountains* form a distinctive mountain range. *The River Nile* is that river and no other. The class-word can be omitted when the specifying word is sufficient to identify the feature: *The Mediterranean* (Sea), *the Pacific* (Ocean), *the Sahara* (Desert), *the* (River) *Ganges*. Note the effect of omitting 'islands' and 'mountains': *the Philippine Islands, the Philippines*; *the Himalaya Mountains, the Himalayas*; *the Rocky Mountains, the Rockies*. The unit noun cannot be omitted when the modifying word by itself is inadequate identification: *the Red, the Indian, the Giants, the British* (as an abbreviation for *the British Isles*) could be applied to too many other things for the meaning to be clear.

87   A signal of specification is not normally felt to be necessary with names of lakes and individual mountains; thus *Everest, Lake Baikal*. But note *the Peak* (**85**) and *the Matterhorn*.

88   It is important, however, that ships should be distinguished one from another: *Is that the 'Queen Elizabeth' or the 'Queen Mary'?* An account of naval manoeuvres in Nelson's day (early nineteenth century) refers first to *the 'Swift' frigate,* then to *the Swift*. (Sailors on board the *Swift*, for whom that vessel was home, spoke of it simply as *Swift*. See **102**.) Railway trains and aeroplanes are now being specified in this way. *The* has long been a signal of specification for inns, taverns and hotels—*the Crown* (Inn), *the Elephant and Castle* (Tavern),[1] *the Grand* (Hotel). Names of newspapers and periodicals are also preceded by *the—The Times, The Lancet, The Asahi, The Mainichi*—whether as an indication that one must be distinguished from another, or to indicate, for example, the one and only *Times*. *The Bible* (literally 'the book') is a solitary member of

---

[1] In South London, mentioned in Shakespeare's *Twelfth Night*.

its class, as is *the Koran*, or *the Odyssey*, or *the Iliad*. But we can borrow a bible, i.e. a copy of *the Bible*, just as we can borrow a '*Hamlet*' or a '*War and Peace*'.

89   One way of tracing the tendencies of living grammar is by observing native speakers in the act of creating their own idiom. I once worked in Crespel Street in Brussels for an organisation that was looking for other premises. We found what we wanted in Avenue Marnix, and referred to it as 'the Marnix building'. Soon, perhaps in imitation of those whose lead we followed socially, we were calling it 'the Marnix'. But our original office remained 'Crespel'. Thus, from Crespel, we would say, 'Are these things going over to the Marnix?'; but, speaking from the new building, 'My books are still over at Crespel.' (See **102**.)

90   It may be in such circumstances that English usage has grown up with apparent inconsistency in the use of the articles, as in other respects. With many of the names used in daily life by English-speakers, there is no way, without becoming intimately acquainted with that life, of telling when convention or fashion or accident will decide whether we say *the Marnix building* or *the Marnix* or just *Marnix*. All three are possible in English: one has to know which happens to have been adopted in each case. The student need not worry about the parochial whims of British or American speakers unless he wishes to make a special study of them. But he needs to know in what ways the language can operate on such occasions. In the case of life in Britain, it operates with the following results:

(*a*) *Buckingham Palace, Hampton Court, St Paul's Cathedral, Victoria Station* (or simply *Victoria*), *London Bridge, Regent Street, Horseferry Road, Covent Garden* (until recently both market and opera house), *Marble Arch*. Note that *the Regent's Park*, named after *the Regent* (**70** (*c*)) was popular a century ago, and that *the Marble Arch* is not dead yet.

(*b*) *The Tower of London* (or *the Tower*), *the Monument* (the one commemorating the Great Fire of London in 1666), *the Strand* (a unit word—cp. *the Peak*, quoted in **87**), *the Edgware Road* (the road leading to Edgware), *the Old Vic* (Theatre), *the British Museum, the London Zoo, the Shakespeare theatre* (cp. **the Shakespeare's theatre*, **68**).

91   One might rationalise some of these usages by arguing, for example, that with *London University* we are not admitting the need for specification—there is only one university in London and this is it; whereas with *the London Library* we have in mind the existence of other libraries, in London and elsewhere, but this is the one we are specifying. Similarly, *Edinburgh University* and *the Edinburgh Festival*. However, when the unit word precedes the proper noun, *the* is used in any case: *The Tower of London, the University of London*, etc. *The* being a mark of distinction, *the University of Oxford* is felt to be more ceremonial than *Oxford University*.

Mass Nouns Used as Unit Nouns

92   Which abstractions and substances are customarily conceived as units in English is a matter of fact, and the student must observe the facts in use. A good modern dictionary will help him here. He will find that *Virtue is its own reward*, that *Patience is a virtue* and that *Faith, hope and charity are virtues*; that we speak of *faiths*, but to mean the ideas in which we have faith, and *charities* to mean not 'acts of charity' but organised objects of charity. We speak of *doubts and injustices*, i.e. matters in which we have doubt, and acts of injustice, but not *justices*, unless we are referring to judges. *Information* and *progress* would only occur in normal English in aspects 1 and 5 **(80)** and so would *advice*. *News* though plural in form, takes a singular verb and also occurs only in aspects 1 and 5. *Weather* is usually found only in the same two aspects, though we find the expression *go out in all weathers*, where it can be used in aspect 2.

'Classifiers' Used with Mass Nouns

93   One example of a substance or material is often indicated in English by 'classifiers', rather as in Chinese. The commonest and most useful classifier is *piece*, which can be used with abstractions as well as substances; e.g. *a piece of paper, of cloth, of wood, of bread, of meat, of advice, of information, of news*. No shape is suggested by *piece*, but a piece of a more definite form can be indicated by *slice, strip, grain, stick, lump, heap, ball, sheet, block*, and similar words in constant household use. We can have *a slice of bread, cake or meat*; *a strip of cloth, of land*; *a grain of rice, of corn*; *a stick of chalk, of dynamite*; *a lump of lead, of coal*; *a heap of earth, of rubbish*; *a ball of wool*; *a sheet of paper, of metal rolled thin*; *a block of wood, of ice*. Colloquially, we can have *a bit* (i.e. a small piece) *of anything*. Some words have their own classifiers: *a loaf of bread, a joint of meat, a rasher of bacon, a clod of earth*. Similarly, we speak of *a blade of grass*; but we can pick out a (single) *hair* from the hair which grows on our heads. *Money* is a mass noun; the corresponding unit noun is *coin*, or *note*, or *pound*, *dollar* etc. All the classifiers mentioned above refer to solids, though we can speak metaphorically of *a sheet of water*, referring to smooth surface. The liquid equivalent of *bit* would be *drop*.

94 When we do find a word for a substance or abstraction used with *a* it is either to indicate *a kind of* that substance or a finished product consisting of it. *A good wine* is a good *kind* of wine; *a bread* is a *kind* of bread, not a loaf. The same could be said of *an iron*, *a paper*, *a cloth*. But also and commonly *an iron* is a household implement; *a paper* is a newspaper, a written report or dissertation, or a set of examination questions; *a cloth* is the finished article spread over a table, or a small piece of cloth for cleaning. Similarly, *a work* is a product of work, a new creation. We speak of *a work of art*, *the works of Dickens*, *the devil and all his works*. Ordinary human beings merely *do a job*, or, if they wish to avoid that humble word, *a piece of work*; more formally they *fulfil a task*. *A play*, too, is a new creation—a story written for acting. A form of play complete in itself would be *a game*.

'People' and Nationalities

95 With its individualistic concept of society, English envisages people only as separate units. If the question asked in **83** were applied to *people*, the answer we would usually expect would be *What are people?* However, *people* can refer either to two or more persons considered together, or to a racial group. *The people* also means 'the general public'. Considered according to the six aspects in **80**, *people* fits into the following scheme:

Aspect	Individual human beings		Racial group
1	person	——	—
2	persons	people	peoples (racial groups in general)
3	a person	——	a people (a racial group)
4	persons	people	peoples (more than one racial group)
5	the person	——	the people (the group, the public)
6	the persons	the people	the peoples (the racial groups)

People is followed by a plural verb, invariably when it means *persons*, and often when it refers to one racial group. *Persons*, instead of *people*, is typical of official English, e.g. *All persons who have not yet registered should do so without delay.*

96   Nationalities present a special problem, and we can only tell from experience or from a detailed reference book what names are appropriate to inhabitants, for example, of China, Egypt, Finland, Scotland, Switzerland, etc (see *A Grammar of Contemporary English*, by Quirk, Greenbaum, Leech and Svartvik, section 4.33). What we are concerned with here is the use of articles before such names. There are three main groups of nationality names:

   (i)   *A German*, plural *Germans;* similarly, *African, American, Russian*, etc.
   (ii) *A Frenchman*, plural *Frenchmen;* similarly *Dutchman, Englishman, Irishman, Scotsman, Welshman.*
   (iii) *A Chinese*, plural *Chinese;* similarly, *Japanese, Portuguese, Swiss.*

There is a further complication: we can say *one Frenchman, two Frenchmen*, etc. referring to individual members of a certain race; or *Frenchmen* or *the French* referring to that race in general. Note the following instances:–

One member	*Two or more members*	*The race as a whole*
An American	Two etc. Americans	Americans *or* the Americans
A Briton	Two etc. Britons	Britons* *or* the British
A Chinese	Two etc. Chinese	Chinese *or* the Chinese
A Dutchman	Two etc. Dutchmen	Dutchmen *or* the Dutch
An Englishman	Two etc. Englishmen	Englishmen *or* the English
A Frenchman	Two etc. Frenchmen	Frenchmen *or* the French
A German	Two etc. Germans	Germans *or* the Germans

   * *Britons* (meaning *the British* as a race) is rarely used today, except in the press. It is remembered in the 18th Century song, still popular, ending *Britons never, never, never, shall be slaves.*

and so on. Then note the difference between each member of the following pairs of sentences:

   [20a]   The French (i.e. Frenchmen in general) drink wine.
   [20b]   The Frenchmen at that table over there are drinking vodka.
   [21a]   The Chinese, as a race, like good food.
   [21b]   The Chinese sitting at that table are not eating anything.
   [22a]   The English (i.e. English people in general) like tea.
   [22b]   The Englishmen at that table over there are drinking saké.

[23a]　The Germans (*or* Germans, i.e. German people in general) drink beer.

[23b]　The Germans at the table are drinking mineral water.

In those sentences, *the French, the Chinese* (in (21a)), *the English* and *the Germans* (in (23a)) have what is called 'generic' reference, whereas *the Frenchmen, the Chinese* (in (21b)), *the Englishmen* and *the Germans* (in 23b)) refer to two or more individual members of the race named.

Unit Nouns Unmarked by 'A' or 'The'

97　Instances of unit-words in aspect 1 (see **80**) are:

(*a*) Notices: *Footpath to beach* (*notice* seen at *holiday resort*).

(*b*) Notes: as in *words* italicised in *brackets* in *line* above and in this note.

(*c*) Signs and labels: *Arrow-head, fifth century* (in a museum), *Strand, Edgware Road* (street signs).

(*d*) Newspaper headlines: *Bride-to-be Abducted at Church Gate.* Here, the absence of articles, besides saving space, tempts the reader to look for the specific details provided in the article below the headline.

(*e*) Telegrams: WIRE DATE CONTRACT SIGNED LETTER FOLLOWS. The receiver of this telegram should know which contract and which date were meant; in any case, the 'letter' that 'follows' would supply the necessary specification.

(*f*) Certain words in constant, communal use, when specification is no longer felt by the community concerned to be necessary: *School begins next Monday. Term ends on December 19th* (spoken as 'December the nineteenth'). *To dine in Hall* (the dining-hall of a college at Oxford or Cambridge). British (and other) people commonly refer to their parliament as *Parliament* (no article); members of trades unions and other associations refer to their own annual conference as *Conference*; and so on. See also **88**.

(*g*) Names of relationships used as proper nouns: *Father* (nominative case) *says we mustn't. Give it to Mother* (objective case). *Thank you, Uncle* (vocative case). *Baby, Nurse* and *Sister* (meaning 'senior nurse') can also be used in this way, in all three cases. Names of certain ranks and titles are used likewise, though now usually in the vocative case only: *Yes, Colonel. Carry on, Sergeant. I'm feeling much better, Doctor. That's all I know, Inspector* (of police); similarly, *Officer* and *Constable* in the police-force. This usage would not apply to persons of rank high above the level of the man in the street. One would therefore speak of *the King, the Duke, the President* (in accordance with **72**), but not say *I'm happy to meet you, Duke.* One could always address an important man as *sir*, or a lady as *madam*.

(*h*) Names of definite appointments. Note: *He is a bank manager*—he is a member of that class. But he is *Manager of the Westminster Bank*. Similarly, *He is President of the Republic, Rector of the University, Director of the Department*. In these last four examples, *the Manager, the President*, etc. are also possible and in fact add a tone of distinction to the title (cp. **72** and **91**). Observe the difference between *He was (the) Minister of Finance* (of that particular country, at that particular date), and *He was a Minister of Finance* (one of a series of Ministers of Finance).

(*i*) In certain types of expression where words are put in couples or in a list: *They became man and wife* (were married). *People worked day and night, in office, field and factory.*

(*j*) With a noun in apposition to another: *Thomas Hardy, author of 'Tess of the d'Urbervilles'*. Omission of *the* in this case is not obligatory.

98   There are many fixed expressions composed of preposition + noun (e.g. *in fact*) or verb + noun (*give way*) in which we are not concerned with a specific example of the concept represented by the noun. Other examples: *in doubt, at ease, in general, at rest, in time, at war, at work*; *do harm, make peace, make progress*. The instances just quoted are of abstractions and it is understandable that they should occur with the zero article. But unit-words can also fit into this pattern when we are concerned not with a particular example of the concept but with, for example,

(*a*) an action communally associated with the object referred to; *go to bed* (to rest), *be (or stay) in bed, get out of bed*; *go to church* (to pray, to attend a service); *go to hospital, be (or stay) in hospital* (for treatment); *go to market* (to buy or sell); *be at office*[1] (working), *go to office* (to work), *be in office* (hold an appointment); *go to prison* (as a punishment); *go to school* (to study or teach); *go to university*.

(*b*) with the class of object, rather than any particular example of it, by which something is conveyed: *to go by bus, by car, by coach, on foot, by plane, by sea, by train*; to send a letter *by hand, by special messenger*;

[1] This usage may not have become generally established, but it is common enough in London, where office-going is an important communal activity (see **97** (*f*) and **99**).

(*c*) with the idea in general, or the thing in the abstract: *at dawn, on edge, in goal, in hand, at night, in person, in question, on record, in reply, at sea.*

99   Such word-groups tend to form when they express a fixed idea that constantly occurs in a community and when it is not felt necessary to specify the object represented by the noun. When one of those nouns is used to refer to a specific object or to express a different idea, then the fixed expression is no longer operative. Thus: *The postman goes to the hospital to deliver letters.* He does not in this case go for treatment; and he goes to a hospital specified by the context in which that statement is made. In *His story is on record* we do not say *where*, but in *Everything he told us is on the record* we refer to the known record of a particular incident. Note the difference between *by sea* **98** (*b*), and *by the sea*, i.e. *beside the sea* (**74**).

100   Specification is sometimes accompanied by a change of preposition, notably from *at* (unmarked, unspecified dimension) to *on* or *in*, where dimension is more clearly indicated (see Chapter 9) e.g. *at sea*, but *on the sea* (on the surface) and *in the sea* (in the water); *at night*, but *in*, or *during*, *the night* (a specific night, or *the night* as distinct from *the day*).

101   It should be noted that the kind of expressions dealt with in **98** must be accepted by the community; that in some situations they are optional (one can say *in spring, summer, autumn, winter* or *in the spring* etc., *go to university* or *go to the university*); while in some situations they have not found acceptance at all (e.g. we say *in bed* but not *on bed, *in chair, or *on chair). On the other hand, in some situations a different pattern has become established: e.g. *go to the theatre to see a play* or *to the station to catch a train*; *in the morning, in the afternoon, in the evening*. In these last examples we find the tendency noted in **74** of marking off known points on the map, either in space (*the theatre/the cinema/the bank*) or in time (*the afternoon/the evening*; *the summer/the winter*).

Man v the Animals

102   Why *man* but *the animals*? *Home is where one starts from* (T. S. Eliot, 'East Coker'). We say, '*This is home. We're at home. Go out, and come home again.*' There is no need to specify which home, or this part of the map as distinct from another. That kind of specification only begins when we venture away from our point of primary concern. But when the point of primary concern becomes the school, as it does with educationists, they can properly ask, '*Should moral education be given at school or in the home?*' (Note the change of preposition, as in **100**.) *Crespel* (**89**) was '*home*'; *the Marnix*, a definite sector of the outside world. Londoners live *in town*, but like to spend their holidays *in the country* or *by the sea*. English-speaking people in Greece go from *Athens*, centre of *Attica*, down to *the Peloponnese*. In Japan, they go from *Tokyo* down to *the Kansai*. It is perhaps typical of man, at least of the English-speaking man, and now of woman, that he, and she, should regard themselves as such a centre, surveying the rest of creation, e.g. *children* (in general) or *the child* (imaginary representation of that class: see **75**), *the animals* and *the birds* (the different classes of animals and birds) as categories of objects in the world outside them.

When is a Noun 'Specified'?

103 When is a noun sufficiently specified for *a* before it to become *the*? In *David Jones is a doctor*, *a doctor* is considered unspecified. David is one of all the doctors in the world. *A doctor* is still unspecified if we add a descriptive adjective, e.g. *good*. All we are then saying is that David is a member of the whole class of good doctors.

104 There are three main conditions in which *a* + noun can be replaced by *the* + noun:

(*a*) when reference is made *back* to something already said, in the following way:

[24]   A doctor and a policeman happened to be standing nearby when the accident happened. The doctor (*i.e. the one just mentioned*) was David Jones.

(*b*) by an adverbial—often in the form of a prepositional phrase— or by a relative clause. Reference is then to something that will follow the noun, e.g.

[25]   The doctor *on duty* was David Jones.
[26]   The doctor *who signed the certificate* forgot to put the date on it.

(*c*) by a superlative or an ordinal number:

[27]   David Jones is *the best* doctor in the district.
[28]   He lives in *the third* house on the left.

105 However, the kind of information provided in **104** is still only sufficient to justify the use of *the* if it enables us to identify *exactly* the person or thing referred to. In saying *He was the doctor on duty that evening* we assume there was only *one* doctor on duty. It would be perfectly correct to say

[29]   David was a doctor on duty that evening,

if we mean that he was *one of those* on duty then. Similarly, we can have *a first prize*, as in

[30]   I have taken part in many competitions but have never won a first prize yet.

On the other hand, any adjective coming before the noun can justify the use of *the* if it enables us to identify the object without doubt. If there are three cups on the table, a white one, a blue one and a brown one, and you ask me which one is mine, either *the white* (*one*), *the blue* (*one*) or *the brown* (*one*) will give you an exact answer.

106 A slightly different use of *the* occurs in cases like *the 'law school, the 'wine trade, the 'coal industry*, where *law, wine, coal* bear the main stress. A university contains several schools or faculties; trade is made up of various trades or branches of commerce; industry has its branches too. *The law school, the wine trade*, etc. refer to one specific branch of the organisation or activity concerned.

107 Similarly, with mass nouns we need to know when a noun is sufficiently specified to justify replacing zero by *the*. The mere insertion of an adjective is not enough. Thus, at university we can study *art—classical art* or *modern art*; or *economics—nineteenth-century economics*, if we like; *history—ancient history, Chinese history, European history*; *law—Roman law*, or some other kind. Note that *European history* refers to European history in general, but *the European history we learnt at school* is specified. The same thing applies to unit nouns in the plural; the mere insertion of an adjective does not justify inserting *the*. Thus, we can import *bicycles—British bicycles*, or *Japanese bicycles*; or *glass, Venetian glass, Czech glass* or any other kind. Again, note the difference between *Venetian glass is beautiful* and *The Venetian glass my mother gave me was wonderful*.

Specification by 'Of'-phrases

108 A phrase beginning with *of* will usually provide sufficient specification to justify the use of *the* before mass nouns or unit nouns in the plural: cp. *Oxford University* but *the University of Oxford* (**91**). Similarly, *Chinese history* but *the history of China*; *nineteenth-century literature* but *the literature of the nineteenth century*.

109   However, an *of*-phrase need not always attract *the*. Compare *the Peace of Versailles* with *peace of mind* i.e. *peace in the mind*, mental peace. Compare *the freedom of university life* (as distinct from the restrictions of life at school) with *freedom of speech*, or freedom to express one's opinions. Similarly, a relative clause after a mass noun may provide the specification that requires *the*. Thus:

[31]   Work can be enjoyable; but the work that factory-workers have to do can be very monotonous.

But relative clauses, too, do not always attract *the*. Compare

[32]   I must attend to work that has accumulated while I have been away

with

[33]   I must attend to the work that has accumulated etc.

Both [32] and [33] are correct: in [32] the speaker is referring to work vaguely, while in [33] he is referring to certain specific tasks and to those only. It is the intuitive or conscious awareness of such subtleties that helps to give good writing precision.

CHAPTER 4

Aspects of Quantity

How the Quantifiers are Used

110 The determiners that indicate aspects of quantity (see **51**) can be used as follows:

With mass nouns, or units plural	*With mass only*	*With units plural only*	*With units singular*
all	a little	both	all
any	much	a few	any
enough		many	each
a lot		several	either
more			every
most			neither
no			no
plenty			some
some			

111 Some of those words can be used with reference to more than two units, others with two only:

More than two	*Two only*
all	both (= the two)
every	——
each	each
some	——
any	either
no	neither

112 (*a*) All the quantifiers can come directly before a noun, though *a lot* and *plenty* must first be followed by *of*. Thus *I'd like some stamps, please, a lot of stamps.*

(*b*) All the quantifiers except *every* and *no* can be used as pronouns, e.g. *Stamps? I haven't any, but George has some. Every one* can be used as a substitute for *every* + noun, and *none* can be used as a substitute for *no* + noun.

(*c*) All the pronoun forms, i.e. *some, any, every one, none* etc. can be used as pre-determiners in the construction:

Pre-determiner		Definite identifier (68)	Noun
some, any		the, this, that	money
every one	+ of +	these, those,	books
none		my, your, his etc.	

After *all* and *both*, the *of* can be omitted. After *both, the* can also be omitted. We can say *all of those* or *all those* (but only *all of them, all of it*). *All* and *both,* as well as *each,* can also be used in these constructions:

[1] They all (= *all of them*) went home.
[2] They all have their jobs to do.
[3] They have all gone.
[4] They are all here. They are all waiting.
[5] I have seen them all (= *all of them*). I have given them all their tickets.

Note the difference between [2], where *have* is a 'full' verb, and [3], where *have* is an auxiliary.

All

113 Suppose two parcels arrive at my house. One parcel contains a large piece of cake, in a solid mass. It is *a piece of cake*, i.e. part of a greater mass, not an object complete in itself. The other parcel contains books, independent units, each a complete whole.

Fig. 7

There we have all the cake and all the books. Note: *All the cake— all of it—is in one box. All the books—all of them—are in another.* The negative of *all* is *not all*, which may mean *almost all* or *only some*. The opposite of *all* is *none*.

Every

114 In saying *all the books*, we have in mind a collection of units, with emphasis on the collection. We can imagine the same books and emphasis on the units: in that case, we refer to *every book*, and say *Every book is in the box.*

All the books

Every book

Fig. 8

Then we have *every book* or *every one of them*. *All v every* is a matter of the collection as a whole v the collection considered as separate units. The double focus in *every*, i.e. the focus on both the unit separately and the units collectively, often leads to sentences like *Everyone was in their place*, where *their* refers not to one person but to many. *Everyone was in his place*, though 'correct' and typical of formal style, can sound pedantic in everyday speech.

Each

115 Consider the books again, not all at once, but one at a time: look at *each book* separately. We could, if space permitted, show each book in a series of diagrams like this.

Fig. 9

The contrast in *every v each* is between the single units considered together and the single units considered one by one. The difference between *every* and *each* was well illustrated in a film of Shakespeare's *Julius Caesar*, in which Mark Antony was addressing the crowd in the market-place after Caesar's death. Paraphrasing Shakespeare's words slightly, Antony was declaring: '*Caesar has left to every man his fields*' (the film showed us all the people cheering and looking joyfully at one another) '*and to each*' (pause: the film gave a close-up of one man after another, looking enquiringly and then congratulating himself, as Antony went on) '*a thousand drachmas.*'

116   Apart from that slight difference in emphasis, *every* and *each* may not only have the same meaning but be interchangeable in sentences on the model of

[6]   Every book (*or* Each book) was by a well-known author.

However, the two words are not always interchangeable:

(*a*) Both *every* and *each* could only be used in the example [6] above if there were three books or more: only *each* would be acceptable if there were no more than two.

(*b*) While we could say *Every one*, or *Each one, was by a well-known author*, we could omit *one* after *each* but not after *every*.

(*c*) We could not replace *each* by *every* in the sentences

[7]   The books cost two pounds each.
[8]   I have given them each their tickets (see **112** (*c*)).

Note the concord in

[9]   Each of them has a ticket.

but

[10]   They have each had their tickets.

Any

117   Now suppose I cut the cake into slices, of different sizes, and say to you, '*Take any of it*'; and suppose I offer you the books saying, '*Take any book you like, any one of them, any of them.*' If you take me at my word, you will choose whatever slice of cake or whatever book or as many slices of cake or as many books or whatever kind of book, you like. You may, if you are greedy, take everything. I am giving you an *unlimited* choice within the whole range; each part of the cake, each book, stands a chance of being selected, thus:

Fig. 10

So *any* indicates one unit, or one number or part or kind, chosen from all; and we can say *any cake, any of the cake, any of it, any book, any books, any one; any two* etc. *Any child could tell you that* means that there is not one child in all the world who would fail to tell you.

118 In *one chosen from all* the emphasis could fall on *one* or on *all*. Hence a statement like *I don't lend my books to any of the students* can be interpreted in two ways. Spoken with strong stress and falling intonation on *any*, it would mean *I don't lend my books to one single student* (emphasis on *one*)—*in fact, I lend them to nobody*. Spoken with a fall-rise intonation on *any* and another rise on *students*, it would mean *I don't lend my books to one or more of all the students* (emphasis on *all*) *but only to one or more of a selected few*.

Some

119 Instead of giving you an unlimited choice, I can divide the parcels up so as to give you one fixed part of the mass or one fixed number of the units, so that you get *'some/sʌm/of the cake* or *some/səm/'cake* and *'some/sʌm/of the books* or *some/səm/'books*.

Fig. 11

Put a piece of paper over Fig. 11, quickly. Can you say exactly what size that piece of cake is, or how many books I have given you? You will probably guess, and you may guess wrong; but whatever the answer is, only one answer is possible. *Some* indicates a fixed though unstated quantity—a limited but unspecified amount of a mass or number of units.

120 In **119,** *some* is used as a quantifier, answering the question *How much?* or *How many?*

As a quantifier, *some* can stand in contrast with *all* or with *none.* The quantity it refers to is usually small, though it could be fairly large as in

[11] A. Are we nearly there yet?
      B. Oh no, we still have some/sʌm/way to go.

Some can mark a contrast between one part of a whole and another, as in

[12] Some/sʌm/people like tea, some/sʌm/prefer coffee, some/sʌm/like plain water.

121 *Some* can also be an identifier, answering the question *What?* or *Which?* Thus:

[13] A. What book can I find that information in?
      B. I don't know; but there must be some/sʌm/book in the library that will tell you.

Contrast that example with *Any book will tell you*: see **117.**

Some v Any

122 *Some* as a quantifier, not *any*, is required in an affirmative statement like

[14] There are some books in my bag. (*There is a fixed though unstated number*);

whereas *any* as a quantifier, not *some*, is required in a negative statement like

[15] I haven't any money.

The negative may be contained in a word other than *not*, e.g. *never, hardly (ever), seldom, rarely*, as in

[16] I seldom have any luck in these competitions;

or it can be carried over from a main clause to a subordinate one, as in

[17] I didn't know you had any brothers and sisters.

In questions, *some* can be used, especially if an affirmative answer is expected; or *any*, if the answer is in doubt:

[18] Would you like some more tea?
[19] I can't find the milk. Did we get any today?

Note that *some* but not *any*, as a quantifier, will occur as a single word answer, as in

[20] A. Is there any bread left?
      B. Some *or* None. (*Any *would be unacceptable here.*)

As an identifier, *any* can always be used in an affirmative statement, as in

[21] Any child can tell you that;

while *some* can be used in a negative, e.g.

[22] Some/sʌm/boy isn't telling the truth.

However, it can be argued that [21] is basically negative, since it means *There isn't any child* (*who can't*), while [22] is basically affirmative since it means *There is some boy* (*who isn't . . .*). In any case, note that the identifier *any* can be used as a single-word answer:

[23] A. Which of these books may I borrow?
      B. (Oh,) any (of them) (*i.e. the choice is unlimited*).

No, None, Not Any

123 Finally, when every piece of the cake is eaten and every book is given away (notice that I said *every* there, since my emphasis is on all the units considered together), then I have *no cake, no book* or *no books* left—I have *none*. Alternatively, we could say, *I haven't any cake, I haven't a book* or *any books*—*I haven't any left*. *N't any* would be more informal than *no*. While the unit noun after *no* may be singular or plural, singular is usual in a case like

[24] There's no telephone in my office,

i.e. when we would expect to find at least one telephone; and plural would occur in a case like

[25]   That poor child has no shoes,

i.e. when more than one shoe would be natural. *None* meaning 'not one of them' is subject to the same kind of double focus as *every*. Though *None of them remains*, with a singular verb, is 'correct', *None of the boys have remembered to bring their books* would be normal and acceptable in conversational style.

Everything, Anything, Something, Nothing

124   *Every* (not *each*), *any*, *some* and *no* can combine with *one*, *body*, *thing* and *where* to produce *everyone*, *everybody* etc. Each of these combinations would be written as one word, except *no one*. *Nothing* is pronounced /nʌθiŋ/. Note that *every* etc. plus *other thing*, *other person*, *other place* are usually replaced by *everything else*, *everyone else*, *everywhere else*, etc. What has been said of the difference between *some* and *any* would also apply to the difference between *something* (*someone*, *somewhere*) and *anything* (*anyone*, *anywhere*). Thus:

[26]   I have something to tell you.

[27]   I haven't anything to say.

[28]   A. What would you like to eat?

       B. (I'd like) something *or* Nothing, thank you *or* Anything.

In B's response, *Anything* cannot refer to quantity (see example [20]) but has a meaning similar to that of *any* in example [23].

(A) Little, (A) Few

125   (*A*) *little* and (*a*) *few*, can be considered as aspects of *some*, with emphasis on the smallness of the amount (little) or of the number (few). *A little* and *a few* suggest a positive quantity—more than none, while *little* and *few* suggest a negative one, almost none. The pattern is similar to that of *to, at, from* (**46**, section 27).

```
    0  1  2  3  4  5  etc.
    ─────────────────►         a little, a few
         None    ×             some
    ◄─────────────────         little, few
```

Thus:

[29]   Don't hurry. We've a little time, a few minutes, yet.

[30]   He rarely speaks. He has little to say. He is a man of few words.

Though (*a*) *few, fewer, fewest*, refer to number (of units), not amount (mass), *less* is becoming increasingly used in everyday speech instead of *fewer*, as in

[31]   There were less than fifty people present.

In any case, *less* would be normal when reference is being made to a sum of money or a distance as in:

[32]   This suit cost less than twenty pounds.

[33]   Our house is less than a hundred metres from the station.

Much, Many

126   The distinction between amount (mass) and number (units) is clearly made by *much* and *many*:

[34]   A. How much bread have we got?
      B. Not much, *or* Too much *or* Not so much as yesterday.

[35]   A. How many potatoes are there?
      B. Not many *or* Too many *or* Not so many etc.

While in short affirmative answers to those questions, 'B' can say *Too much* or *Too many*, we would not hear **We've got much*: instead (*We've got*) *a lot* or *plenty* or *a good deal* would be normal. *There are many* would be more acceptable than **There's much*; but, even so, *There are a lot* or *plenty* or *a good many* would be more idiomatic. However, affirmative *much* and *many*, not modified by *too* or *so*, would be perfectly all right in more formal style, as in *There is much to be said for this proposal.* Cp. footnote to **307**, and see **46** 29.

Degrees of Quantity

127   Imagine we are emptying, then filling, a container with an

QUANTITY

Scale	*How much is there?*		*How many are there?*
6	not much		not many
4	less		fewer
2	very little	hardly any	very few
Empty 0		——— ~~NONE~~ ———	
2			
4	a little		a few
6		more	some
8		not enough	several
10		not quite enough	
12		enough	
14		a lot	
16			
18	a good deal		a good many
Full 20		———	
22	too much		too many

amount (say, of flour or water) or with a number (say, of books). The words on the left of the vertical line in the table above refer to amount; those on the right to number; those in the middle to either. Note that *any* cannot appear on that table: *any amount** or *any number* could refer to every point on the side. But *hardly any* can appear as it means *almost none*.

* The phrase *any amount* is often used to mean that the amount is very large— almost unlimited (see **46** 9) as in:

(36) Are you looking for paper? There's any amount of it in that cupboard.

Book as a Mass, Cake as a Unit; All v Whole

128   The two parcels (**113**) might have contained one large book and a box of small cakes. We can then say

all (of) the book	all (of) the cakes
—	every *or* each cake
any of the book	any (single) cake, any cakes
some of the book	some of the cakes
none of the book	none of the cakes
much of the book	many of the cakes
a little of the book	a few of the cakes

[37]   I haven't read all (of) the book (*or* the whole book) yet.

[38]   A. Have you understood *any* of the book?
B. I've understood a little of it, but not much (of it).

Note:

[39]   Is there any egg on my face? (see **55**).

Note also that *little* in *a little cake* can be either an adjective, meaning *small* (one little cake) or a determiner, meaning *a small quantity of*, as in *May I have a little (of that) cake, please?*

129   Before certain nouns referring to periods of time, not only *of* but also *the* may be omitted after *all*, as in *We travelled all day* and *all night*. Note the difference between *all day* (i.e. *the whole day*) and *every day* (all the days in a limited or unlimited period). *All morning, all evening, all week* are also current, especially in American English.

Both, Either, Neither

130   See **111**. The distinction between *both*, meaning *the two*, and *all*, presents no difficulty. But as *any* presents such a constant problem, it is helpful to see it in contrast with *either*, thus:

[40] You can't have either of these two books—not this, nor that one.

[41] You can't have any of these three (four, five) etc.—not this, nor that, nor that and so on.

[42] Either of these two roads will take you to London.

[43] Any of these three (*etc.*) will take you there.

Similarly, *none* can be seen in contrast with *neither* (where the same option between singular and plural verb is open):

[44] Neither of the two men was (*or* were) present.

[45] None of the three (*etc.*) was (*or* were).

CHAPTER 5

The Tenses

ASPECTS OF ACTIVITY

131 In what are generally called the tenses, we are concerned with aspects of activity and of time. Time itself might be regarded as an aspect of activity, insofar as it is only in terms of events that time can be measured.

132 English-speakers see activity from several points of view. To understand its expression in the English verb system, we must think of:

(*a*) the general idea of an act, not containing any of the distinctions referred to in the rest of this paragraph;

(*b*) the act seen as accomplished and as a completed whole;

(*c*) the act seen as uncompleted, as having begun and being still in progress. The difference between (*b*) and (*c*) is therefore comparable to that between *all* and *some*;

(*d*) the act performed once;

(*e*) the act performed repeatedly; a whole series of acts, the series seen as a whole;

(*f*) a partial, uncompleted series of acts; the acts being performed temporarily rather than permanently.

133 (*a*) We can compare the general idea of the act (**132** (*a*)) with the general concept referred to by a noun as in **56**, **57**, and **80** aspect 1, where the zero article is required.

(*b*) The act seen as a whole could be illustrated like this:

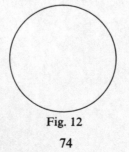

Fig. 12

(*c*) The action in progress, like this:

Fig. 13

There, the thin line represents time, the thicker line represents action in progress: this is the progressive aspect, expressed by *be* + the *-ing* form of the verb.

(*d*) The act performed once, like this:

Fig. 14

(*e*) A series of acts, viewed as a whole, thus:

Fig. 15

This can be compared with the illustration for *every* in **114**.

(*f*) A partial or uncompleted series of acts, like this:

Fig. 16

and an uncompleted series never stopping, like this:

Fig. 17

This is, again, progressive aspect, expressed by *be + -ing*.

134   Examples of **132** and **133**:

(*a*)   [1]   Tell a lie? That's something he would never do.
(*b*)   [2]   I tell you it's true. (*I tell you, definitely, now.*)
(*c*)   [3]   Listen carefully to what I'm telling you. (*Listen while the telling is in progress; I haven't finished yet.*)
(*d*)   [4]   I see a ship.
(*e*)   [5]   I see my neighbour on the train every day.
(*f*)   [6]   A. I'm playing tennis every day this week (*partial series*).
        B. But you're always playing tennis (*series that never stops*).

You will see that the progressive aspect is used in examples [3] and [6].

135   Another way of illustrating these aspects of activity would be:

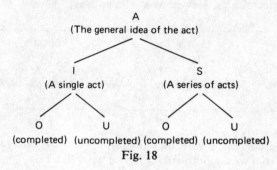

Fig. 18

136   Take *I go* as an example of **135**:

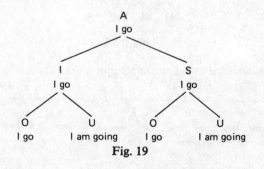

Fig. 19

137   A, in Figs. 18 and 19 represents the general concept;
I, represents the single act;
I O, the single act completed;
I U, the single act uncompleted;
S, the series;
S O, the series completed;
S U, the series uncompleted.

Note that *I go* is used for the whole scheme except **I U** and **S U**: in other words, we say *I go* until and unless we are concerned with the uncompleted act or series, when we can use *I am going*, if it is on *the act, or series, in progress* that we wish to place our emphasis.

138   I repeat 'until and unless we are concerned with' that aspect. What is important is not so much the objective fact as the *aspect* of the fact that the speaker has in mind and wishes to express. For example:

(*a*) In saying *I read in bed for half an hour before I turn out the light*, I refer to a series (of acts) which happens to be incomplete, insofar as I have not given up the habit of reading in bed; but it is not that fact that I wish to emphasise. I am viewing the series as a whole without wishing to draw attention to the idea of **132** (*f*). Similarly, in **132** (*e*), *The River Danube flows into the Black Sea*, we are not concerned with the fact that the Danube is in *process* of flowing or that it *never stops*. We *could* be so concerned and say *The Danube is flowing unusually fast today* or *It is for ever flowing and emptying its waters into the sea*. In *The Danube flows*, etc., we see the phenomenon as a whole without those particular distinctions.

(*b*) In saying *I'm telling you* in **134** [3], I am concerned with the process of telling and with the incompletion of it. My telling may (or may not) be accomplished. If it is, that is irrelevant and is not the aspect to which I want to draw your attention.

(*c*) In reporting two uncompleted actions, we may wish to emphasise the progress of one but not of the other; e.g. *As I stand here, the procession is entering the hall*. It would be vain of me, besides giving the impression that the procession was small and its entrance hasty, if I said *As I am standing here, the procession enters the hall*, though grammatically that is not wrong. Both verbs could take the **O** form and both the **U** in that sentence. But notice the first example given, which is an actual quotation from a radio commentary.

139   Note that the uncompleted act may eventually be finished, or not. In saying *I'm putting my pen on the desk*, i.e. in describing an action in progress, not stating my intention (see **150**), I ought to be concentrating on the gradual movement of hand and pen through the air before they have reached the desk. They may get there, or they may not. It happens to be in my power to stop them. I U can therefore be easily applied to a voluntary act.

140 It may be convenient to teach beginners that the difference between *I'm going* and *I go* is that the former refers to an act performed at the time of speaking, the latter to the act performed habitually. Unfortunately, the difference between *I go*, as an expression of I O, and *I'm going*, as an expression of S U, is also that *I go* in *that* sense refers to an act performed at the time of speaking, while *I'm going* can refer to habitual action. Admittedly, there are many examples of I U in which the predominant idea is one of 'activity now' e.g.

[7]   (I can't understand you)—are you trying to speak English?

Examples of this kind could be compared with ones in which the predominant idea is that of the act performed habitually, e.g.

[8]   Do you speak English at home?

In those examples, the change of verb-form makes it clear that in *are you trying* I mean *at this moment*, while in *do you speak* I mean *usually*. But in linking *are you trying* with *at this moment*, and *do you speak* with *usually* and generalising accordingly, we are reasoning from only part of the evidence. It is quite possible to say, as I do now,

[9]   I stop work at this moment—I'm usually feeling pretty tired by this hour of night.

141 The difference between momentary action and habitual activity is indeed expressed in English by a change of verb-form, but only incidentally in certain types of usage. The difference may be underlined by adverbial expressions such as *at this moment*, or *regularly, often, sometimes, always*. *Now* is not a good example of such an adverb since it can be used for regular activity as well as momentary action, completed as well as uncompleted, e.g.

[10]   Now I put down my pen, I O
[11]   Now I am looking out of the window, I U
[12]   Now I write all my letters myself—(I used to dictate them), S O
[13]   Now I am writing twenty pages a day—(last year I could only do six). S U

It can also be used with the Past tense and with reference to the future:

[14]   I saw him just now. Now we'll stop.

Physical and Mental Activity, Sensory and Mental Perception

142   Just as some of the things we talk about can be imagined more easily in the mass than as units, and vice versa (see **81**), so some of our actions are more easily imagined as completed acts than as uncompleted processes. On the other hand, the uncompleted state is more easily imagined with some actions than with others. The commentator on the football match (**21**) saw the game as a series of accomplished acts; e.g.

[15]   Johnson passes to Roberts, Roberts to Watkins, Watkins takes it forward, oh he slips past the centre half beautifully, he shoots

—all perfect examples of **I O**. Watching a boat race, the commentator is, by the nature of the event, more conscious of movement in progress; e.g.

[16]   Oxford are rowing splendidly—one—two—three—four— they're just coming in sight of Hammersmith Bridge. Ah— Cambridge are increasing their pace

—all **I U**. Here the reader must again be warned against generalising from incidental factors. The movements of football may be quicker, those of rowing may take longer; but the essential factors determining the usage of the verb-form is not speed, or length of duration, but rather the fact that the speed makes the spectator more aware of the completed act, the duration more aware of the action in progress.

143   Verbs referring to physical activity (example [17] below) or to mental activity [18], to physical sensation [19], or to a process [20], that can last a considerable time and thus have duration, are often used in **I U**. Examples:

[17]   (Please be quiet.) I'm writing an important letter.
[18]   I'm considering whether to send a telegram instead.
[19]   My head is aching terribly.
[20]   You're getting tired.

We can easily imagine ourselves in the middle of the act of writing a letter. We can stop the action, and leave it uncompleted, whenever we like. It is therefore a good idea to introduce progressive aspect with verbs of that kind. On the other hand, it is not easy to imagine ourselves in the middle of the act of closing a book, switching on a light or opening a door. That is why I said in **20** that *I'm opening the door*, as a commentary on an action performed at the time of speaking, is unnatural. With verbs like *open* (*a door*), *switch on* (*a light*), *hit*, *jump*, *bark* and so on, the progressive aspect only makes sense if one is referring to repeated acts of opening, switching, hitting, etc.

144   Similarly, it is difficult (though for a scientist not impossible) to catch oneself in the middle of a single act of *seeing* or *hearing*. *To see* or *to hear* is to receive a sensory impression. The reception of the impression is an involuntary act: we cannot normally prevent the completion of it. Thus, as we commonly say in English, *you see—or you don't* (*see*). Yet sometimes it is possible for us to perceive the reception of a visual image in an unfinished state. Wearing the wrong spectacles or having dined not wisely but too well, *I might be seeing double*. Such occurrences of *see* in **I U** may be rare, but they help to explain why *see* is normally found only in the completed aspect. Yet in **S U** *see* would occur as frequently as any other verb, since we have no difficulty in imagining an uncompleted series of the acts of perception; e.g.

[21]   'I'm seeing too many pictures,' said Sue at the exhibition. 'I can't look at any more.'

145   In contrast with *seeing*, the voluntary act of *looking* (*at something*) is easy to imagine in **I U**. Looking at something is like focusing a camera. It can go on for some time: it is physical activity having duration. Seeing something is more like taking a snapshot; once we have pressed the button, we cannot stop the shutter opening and leaving an impression on the film.

146.   Parallel with *see v look* (*at*) is *hear v listen* (*to*). *Smell*, *taste* and *feel* can express both voluntary action and sensory impression and correspond with both *look* (*at*) and *see* accordingly, as in:

[22]   A. Why are you feeling the radiators?
B. To see if the heating is on. I feel rather cold. Yes. The radiator feels quite cold (i.e. I feel cold when I touch it).

147   When we feel cold, we receive an impression through the senses. When we know what the temperature is, we register a mental impression; and that experience, too, is difficult to imagine in its uncompleted state. We can *be finding out* what the temperature is; but, again, *we either know, or we don't. You remember, or you don't. Know, remember, forget, think, believe, suppose, want, like, love, doubt, hope, wish*, are therefore, like *see* and *hear*, very unlikely to occur in the progressive aspect. Note the difference between each member of the following pairs:

[23]   (a) Please be quiet. I'm thinking (*mental activity*).
       (b) I think you're right (*mental impression*).
[24]   (a) The jury is considering its verdict (*mental activity*).
       (b) We consider the prisoner guilty (*mental impression*).

148   Here, the teacher must distinguish between helpful advice and absolute statement. He would be justified in advising his pupils not to use *know, remember*, etc. in the *-ing* form of the verb until they are more advanced. He would be wrong in making them learn a 'rule' to the effect that these words are not used in the progressive form at all. Just as all nouns in English can, potentially, fill all the six positions in **80,** so all verbs (except the modals: see Chapter 6) can, potentially, fill all the positions in **135.**

Psychological Subtleties

149   Since we are concerned in this book with the connection between grammatical form and what we have in mind, it is not surprising that in many of the problems we are discussing there are psychological subtleties. The student can fairly easily understand the difference between *I'm thinking* (mental activity) and *I think* (mental impression: see **147**). He may be more puzzled to hear *I'm thinking you're right*. That can be perfectly 'correct' if the speaker is deliberately using the marked form to suggest that a certain conclusion is forming itself in his mind but is not yet final. Thus *I think you're right* is more definite (besides being safer for the student to imitate) than *I'm thinking you're right*. Similarly, *I'm liking my work*, instead of the normal and more decided *I like it*, suggests that the process of becoming adjusted to it is still going on; or it might mean that I am lingering over its delights. *What are you wanting now?* suggests that you have not made up your mind *what* you want, or that you are in a perpetual state of wanting something you do not have. Then consider the difference between the following:

[25]   (a) I hope you will come and have lunch with me.
       (b) I am hoping you will come and have lunch with me.

Both are right; but they are not equal in the effect they might have on the hearer. Native speakers who select (*a*) rather than (*b*), or vice versa, may be quite unaware that they do, and unable to explain *why* they do. Any explanation one can offer might be drawn from purely personal associations. My own explanation is that a busy, self-important man might feel (*a*) to be too presumptuous, and refuse the invitation, but (*b*) flatteringly deferential and accept; while someone else to whom that invitation was given might feel (*a*) to be definitely meant, and accept with pleasure, but (*b*) to be uncertain and not sufficiently pressing. The speaker's attitude to his audience—dictatorial or deferential, positive or uncertain—can be an important factor in these cases. However, the basic factor in the above examples is not the positiveness, the uncertainty, or whatever it may be in the speaker's attitude, but his conception of the action as whole, as accomplished (*hope*), or partial, in progress or continuing (*hoping*).

I am Leaving Tomorrow

150   One such subtlety that has become stereotyped and commonly adopted is the use of the uncompleted aspect to indicate action which is about to begin or is due to take place in the future. Thus *we're starting* can mean either that action has begun and is in progress, or that action is about to begin or has been planned, that the required impetus has been given, so that the process has in a sense begun already. Note

[26]   I am leaving the country tomorrow and will be abroad for six weeks.

This example provides a contrast between (*am*) (*leav*)*ing* and *will* + infinitive, and we must discuss this later both as an aspect of time **177** and as a question of mood (Chapter 6). It illustrates an aspect of activity insofar as it suggests and emphasises the idea that I have, or someone else has, decided or arranged that I shall leave the country, and the process has in that sense begun, though I do not see it yet as completed—in fact, it may not *be* completed. Note that the terse, businesslike speaker might see the act as completed, and announce firmly *I fly to New York tomorrow*; or, like Julius Caesar, *Tomorrow I cross the Rubicon*. The **O** form can also be used when the speaker's plans are determined for him: *According to schedule I leave at seven in the morning*.

151   As we are seldom so confident that the future will be fulfilled, the U form is commoner than the O form when the Present tense-form is used with future reference. Yet either may occur in the same situation. Referring to future time, one can say *The ship sails at three* (**I O**) or *The ship is sailing at three* (**I U**). It is commonly believed that the latter way of referring to the future is restricted to verbs indicating movement from one place to another. It occurs frequently as an indication of a planned movement; but it can be applied to any situation subject to human control; e.g. *We're discussing your case on Friday* (that item is on the agenda of our meeting). However, we could not say **I'm sneezing in a moment* or **It's raining tomorrow*, since sneezing and raining are not subject to human planning. Moreover, *I'm knowing the result tomorrow* would be rare, such an act of perception being difficult to imagine in an uncompleted state (**147**). Nevertheless, we can say *I'm seeing the doctor on Tuesday* (i.e. I have made an appointment and the process has therefore begun). With acts of perception the **O** form is possible, provided such acts are subject to plan, e.g. *We hear the results tomorrow* (that is when they are due to be published).

152 We frequently find the pattern (*I am*) *going to* (*leave*) (*tomorrow*), especially in colloquial English. If the essential factor in the (*I am leav*)*ing* pattern is the idea that a process has started in the sense that some event has been planned, the essential factor in the (*I am*) *going to* (*leave*) pattern is a focus on some present factor which the speaker feels certain will lead to a future event. The 'present factor' can be decision, intention or preparation, or it can be an obvious symptom of what the future will bring. The (*I am*) *going to* (*leave*) pattern allows the speaker to state separately the preparation for the event and its possible accomplishment. (Here note how accomplishment is expressed by the infinitive, to *leave*; and cp. **282**.) The accomplishment, of course, is imagined, not actual, and may not result. Examples:

[27]   I am going to write to him soon.

This suggests an arrangement as well as intention, so *I am writing* is also possible here.

[28]   You're going to break that chair if you're not careful.

The speaker sees signs of what will happen and is sure of the result. You do not intend to break the chair, and no one has arranged that you will do so: *You're breaking* would therefore be wrong in this context.

[29]   I'm going to sneeze in a moment. (*The signs are clear—I know what will happen.*)

[30]   It's going to rain this evening. (*Comment as in* [29].)

[31]   We're going to understand this eventually.

It will be seen from examples [28], [29], [30] and [31] that the (*I am*) *going to* (*leave*) pattern can be used when the (*I am leav*)*ing* pattern cannot. This may explain the very frequent use in conversation of the former, which is often chosen mechanically when the latter would be equally acceptable. The question of *am leaving/am going to leave v future* will be discussed under *Aspects of time* in **177**. Meanwhile, *am leaving* (*tomorrow*) *v am going to leave* could be expressed as *process imagined as begun in the sense that preliminary decisions, plans or arrangements have been made, v present factors, e.g. personal intentions or objective symptoms, imagined as leading to a completed act.*

ASPECTS OF TIME

153   I O, I U, S O and **S U** can be combined with nine aspects of time, and the resultant combinations are expressed in the various tense-forms. Aspects of time depend on the speaker's point of primary concern in the natural order of events, and on the direction of his vision from the standpoint he adopts. (My nine aspects of time correspond exactly with the nine-part time-scheme on page 28 of D. A. Wilkins's *Notional Syllabuses* (1976).)

154   We might illustrate the natural order of events by a row of numbers, as on the score-board for the game of billiards:

Fig. 20

The arrows on the scoreboard move horizontally and mark the scores of the two players or teams. Let us suppose that the numbers represent happenings, that the top arrow is Time (T) and the bottom the speaker's point of primary concern (SPPC). T moves regularly forward, as if by clock-work. SPPC may keep pace with it, be behind it, or in front of it. T remains pointing vertically downwards. SPPC can swing like the needle of an electrical instrument, so as to point backwards or forwards, at any angle, from whatever position it occupies.

Unlimited Time: Present Tense

155   In the first aspect of time, the 'game' has not begun and neither of the arrows is 'in play'. Time, here, is unlimited; undivided; or it does not matter; we are concerned with timelessness.

[32]   The sea breaks eternally onto the shore.   (**O**)
[33]   The earth is constantly revolving on its axis.   (**U**)

Breaks and *is revolving* are in the Present tense. We regard all time as present until we feel the need to mark some of it off as past or yet to come.

Present Time: Present Tense

156   The second aspect is present time as distinct from past or future. Here the arrows have moved into play and the scores are equal.

Fig. 21

The speaker's attention is focused on an action performed at the time when he is commenting on it. SPPC can be pointing straight towards T, in which case the speaker is commenting on something happening at the very moment of utterance:

[34]   A. Watch me. I put a cross here. X   (**I O**)
       B. I'm watching you. What are you doing that for?   (**I U**)

B is continuing to watch A to see what he will do next. SPPC can also swing backwards and forwards so as to cover a range of activity and events both before and after T. The speaker is then considering something that has actually happened as well as something that he imagines will take place. Thus:

[35]   My sister lives *in England*.   (**I O**)
[36]   I *usually* get up *at seven*.   (**S O**)
[37]   I am learning *Arabic*; and   (**I U**)
[38]   I'm getting *up at six this week to revise for an examination*.
       (**S U**)

A commonly used example of **S U** occurs in an utterance like *John*

has left school and is already going to the university, i.e. he is already
a university student. SPPC can swing so far backwards and forwards
that it covers an unlimited range, which is what we have in **155**.
But the range we are concerned with in **156** is limited, though not
necessarily defined: it is *now* as distinct from *then* (past) and *then*
(future).

157   The previous paragraph could be summarised in this way:

Fig. 22

The horizontal line corresponds with the row of numbers in Fig. 21;
the vertical line with the line made by the two arrows. The shaded
part of Fig. 22 represents the present period: its limits can be close
together or far apart. They can be so close as to meet at the *point
now*, the momentary present. Or they can extend on either side of
the *point now* so that the *period now* overlaps with both past and
future. Thus, while the events in example [34] take place at the
point now, those in [35]–[38] are true of part of the past and of
the future, and may be true of the present moment. Whether the
speaker's attention is focused on *point now* or *period now*, he will
use the Present tense, the tense that was also used in **155**.

Pre-present Time: Present Perfect

158   The third aspect of time is pre-present, leading up to the
present moment. Here, SPPC is still at the same point as T; but
while the T arrow remains pointing vertically downwards, the SPPC
arrow points backwards into pre-present time. In other words, the
speaker is concerned with a period of time before and ending at
point now. He is not concerned with a *specified* time before now;
if he were, SPPC would be behind T, not level with it. The pre-
present may begin anywhere in the past, no matter how long ago.
However, the speaker has a natural tendency to give more attention
to that part of the period which is nearest his viewpoint, i.e. to the
recent past: hence the darker shading in Fig. 23. The beginning of
the pre-present period may or may not be mentioned: it is often

marked by *since*, as in *We've been here since Friday*. This aspect of time is called the perfective and the verb form that expresses it is called the Present Perfect.

Fig. 23

159 We can move the SPPC arrow in different ways. Either it can point vaguely towards some time within the pre-present, in which case the speaker is concerned with activity occurring at some unspecified time *before* now. Or it can move progressively from a backward-pointing position to a completely vertical one, in which case the speaker is concerned with activity continuing throughout the pre-present period *till* now. In either case, *it is the pre-present period that is his basic interest*; and it is this that determines his use of the Present Perfect. As the Present Perfect is not concerned with specified past time, it is not normally[1] used with past time adverbials (e.g. *yesterday, last year*: see **165**); though it can naturally be used with *till now, by now, so far* and the more formal *hitherto*.

160 Examples:

Activity at unspecified time before now

    [39] A. Have you ever been to Mexico (at any time, yet)?
           B. Yes, I've been there once (*time unspecified*). **(I O)**
           C. I've never had a chance to go yet.

Note the use of *yet* with the Present Perfect in questions and in the negative; and the use of *ever*, meaning at any time. The scope of *ever*, like that of *any* (**117**), is unlimited: the limited but unspecified *once* could be compared with *some* (**119**).

    [40] A. Do you know this village?
           B. I know it well. I've lived here. **(I O)**

[1] Examples of the Present Perfect with past time adverbials may occasionally be found. But the student is not advised to imitate them.

Note that in [39] B is not in Mexico; and in [40] B no longer lives in that village.

[41]   A. Why are your hands so dirty?
       B. I've been working in the garden.   (I U)
[42]   Who is that man? I've seen him several times.   (S O)
[43]   You wouldn't recognise Athens now.
       They've been building blocks of flats everywhere.   (S U)

Activity continuing till now

[44]   I've lived here $\begin{cases} \text{since 1974.} \\ \text{for the last twelve years.} \end{cases}$ (I O)

Compare [44] with [40]. The addition of *since 1974* (i.e. from that point of time in the past) and *for the last twelve years* (i.e. throughout that period) implies that my living here has continued till now and I live here still. But even if I am living here still, I do not use the Present tense in [44], nor in [45], [46], [47], because in those examples I am primarily concerned with occurrences within the pre-present period.

[45]   I've been learning Arabic $\begin{cases} \text{since March.} \\ \text{for six months.} \end{cases}$ (I U)
[46]   I've always got up at seven (and still do).   (S O)
[47]   I've been playing tennis every day this week so far.   (S U)

Note the emphasis on the last phase of the pre-present in

[48]   I've just finished another page.

161 Action completed before now will generally produce effects that are noticeable now, e.g.

[49]   A. You *do* look clean.
       B. Yes, I've just had a hot bath.

However, to understand how the Present Perfect operates the student must consider the aspect of time described in **158** and Fig. 23 and not assume that we use the Present Perfect simply because a result is evident. If he starts from that assumption, he will soon discover (*a*) that the Present Perfect is used when there is no result at all and even when a noticeable result is contrary to what might have been expected, as in

[50]   Look at you! You've just had a bath and now you're filthy;

and (*b*) that present evidence may be associated with a tense-form other than the Present Perfect:

[51]   Here are the burglar's footmarks—he came into the house through that window.

162   Uncompleted action in the pre-present period might (*a*) be interrupted before now; or (*b*) continue until now; or (*c*) being uncompleted, continue through the present. Thus, applying Fig. 13 (**133** (*c*)) to Fig. 23 (**158**), we have

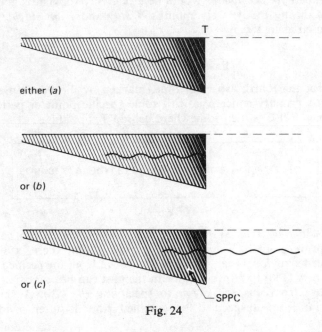

Fig. 24

Examples:

(*a*)   [52]   Who has been sitting in my chair (and is no longer in it)?

[53]   It's been raining, but it's stopped now.

(*b*)   [54]   I'll take the wheel now—you've been driving for four hours.

(*c*)   [55]   We've been learning English for ten years (and are learning it still).

In any case, in (*a*), (*b*) or (*c*), what the speaker is primarily concerned with is the action in progress before now, i.e. in the shaded part of Fig. 23.

163 When the speaker has in mind activity that started before now and wishes to emphasise that it is still continuing, he will use the Present tense (see Fig. 22). Thus, if he wants us to know that he has lived here till now and that he lives here still, he will say *This is where I live*. What he cannot do in English is to combine *I live* with *since* (*a certain date*) or with *for* (*a certain period*), as those phrases are associated with the Present Perfect: example [44]. *I stay*, or *I am staying, here for six months* would be a reference to what is going to happen during the next six months, *I stay* and *I am staying* then being used as in **150**.

Past Time: Past Tense

164 For the fourth aspect of time, marked by the Past tense, the speaker's primary concern is with some specific point or period in past time. SPPC is then somewhere behind T, like this:

Fig. 25

The distance between SPPC and T does not matter: it can be very great or very small. The important thing is that there is a gap, however narrow, between the two. The move from unspecified time before now (**158**) to a specific time in the past can be compared with the move from unspecifying *a* to specifying *the* (**76**). A shift of viewpoint from unspecified to specified time is often made in English.

[56] A. I know this village. I've lived here. (See [40].)
      B. Oh, when was that?
      A. It was fifteen years ago.
[57] Pussy cat, pussy cat, where have you been?
      I've been to London to see the Queen.
      Pussy cat, pussy cat, what did you there?[1]
      I frightened a little mouse under a chair.

165 When SPPC is in time past, the fact is usually indicated by some adverbial expression, e.g. *yesterday, last year, in 1974, fifteen*

---

[1] For *What did you there?*, modern English would of course say *What did you do there?*

years ago. Ago marks a time in the past measured back from now, a time that becomes SPPC. *Ago* therefore requires the Past tense, just as *since* in example [44] required the Present Perfect. Specification of time past can also be made by a temporal clause, e.g. *when I was at school*, or by some other device that helps to fix the time when the event occurred, e.g. *there* in example [57].

166 The Past tense is thus a signal of specification of past time, just as *the* is a signal meaning that the speaker is referring to a specified object (**68**). But though the point or period in past time is usually indicated by something (e.g. an adverb) in the context, it is not always so indicated. Consider the following episode from real life. One morning, just before it was time for my family to get up, my wife and I both heard a sound as of footsteps going downstairs. We asked each other, '*What was that?*' both thinking of the noise we had heard a moment before. A minute later our son Peter appeared at the door of our room with the newspaper. My wife and I spoke simultaneously:

Myself: *Oh, it's you. Good, you've brought the paper.*
My wife: *Oh, it's you. You went down for the paper.*

I used the Present Perfect, my wife the Past. Both were 'right' in the circumstances. But there is a difference in meaning insofar as there was a difference in our points of view, and this would have become apparent had our talk proceeded, as it well might have done, thus:

Wife (to me): *All you think about is your newspaper.*
Self: *You worry too much. Who did you think it was?*

Chiefly interested in the paper before me, I had made the point *now* my primary concern and used the Present Perfect accordingly. Peter's mother, with her mind still on the moment in the past when she had heard steps on the stairs, had made *that* her primary concern.

167 The example just given should explain:

[58] Who broke the window?

The speaker has registered the fact that now it is broken, but he is no longer interested in *now*. What he wants to know is how the accident happened *when* it happened.

[59] Did you have a good journey? (*I'm glad to see you—you know that. I am now thinking of the time in the past when you were on your way here.*)

In both those cases, Present Perfect would be equally acceptable; e.g. *Oh, who has broken the window?* (I don't want to know how it happened; the fact is that it is broken, and I'm asking who is responsible.) Similarly, with *today, this morning, this afternoon*, etc., both the Past tense (*it happened*) and the Present Perfect (*it has happened*) are possible, according to whether SPPC is point now or an earlier time in the period in question. Note:

(Present   [60]   Have you been very busy today (*during the period*
Perfect)   *before now*)?

           [61]   I have seen him this morning. I've just seen him
                  (*at an unspecified time*).

(Past   [62]   Your letter reached me this morning. (*Someone*
tense)   *brought it at a definite moment earlier in the*
                  morning; or this morning if the morning has
                  passed.) It arrived just now (*i.e. a moment ago*).

           [63]   It was terribly hot in town today (but it is cooler
                  out here in the country, now).

168   Notice how the Present Perfect and the Past tense are used with *since*:

[64]   Since I heard her sing, I have always admired her.
[65]   Since he was in the army, he has been in much better health.
[66]   Since we have lived here, we have made many friends.
[67]   Since he has been in the army, we have seen him only twice.

In [64], *I heard* occurred at a point of past time which marks the beginning of the pre-present period; and in [65], he was in the army during a period of past time, since when he has been in better health. In [66] and [67] our living here and his being in the army extend throughout the whole pre-present period. The present perfect can only be used in a *since*-clause with verb referring to activity that can continue throughout a period of time.

169   As in [63] the Past tense can (but does not necessarily) indicate that former conditions no longer exist. Thus *He was an excellent chairman* suggests that he is not chairman now. *He was a wonderful man* suggests he is dead. Other examples: *Where were you born? I was born at . . .*; and *We enjoyed our stay immensely* (our stay ended, say, yesterday), but *We have enjoyed our stay* (which is now ending).

170   The difference between the pre-present and the past is thus a matter of *unspecified time before now* v *specified time in the past, detached from the present*; and the Past tense could be illustrated like this:

Fig. 26

The *point* or *period then* can move forwards as a series of events is reported, e.g. *Caesar came, (then) he saw, (then) he conquered.*

171 **I O**, **I U**, **S O**, and **S U** (see Fig. 18 in **135**) can be applied to the Past tense as to the Present. **I O** can be applied (and often is) to a single act in past time; **S O** to a series of acts or to past habit; **I U** to uncompleted action; and **S U** to a partial series of acts. Examples:

Events occurring at a point of time

[68]   The accident happened at 10.15 this morning.   (**I O**)
[69]   Several people were standing there at the time.   (**I U**)

Events occurring throughout a period

[70]   I lived in England when I was a boy.   (**I O**)
[71]   I got up early in those days.   (**S O**)
[72]   I was having breakfast (when he arrived).   (**I U**)
[73]   I was then getting up at six o'clock every day to prepare for my exams.   (**S U**)

172 **I O** extending over a period, and **S O**, as in examples [70] and [71], can be expressed by *used to*, when emphasis falls on the idea of an act continued or repeated over a period *in the past*, not in the present; e.g.

[74]   I used to live in England (but I don't now).
[75]   I used to get up early (now I'm not so energetic).

This emphatic marking would normally only occur once in a short sentence, thus:

[76]   I used to get up early when I went to school.

Nor would it occur when the length of duration of the past habit is specified: thus, *used to go* could not replace *went* in *I went swimming every day for six years*, but it could replace *went* in *I went swimming every day*.

Pre-past Time: Past Perfect

173   In our fifth aspect of time, the pre-past, SPPC in Fig. 26 is now pointing backwards, and the pattern in Fig. 23 is applied to Fig. 26, thus:

Fig. 27

174   Examples:

Activity before then

[77]   A. I hear you went to India last year. Had you ever been there before?
B. Yes, I'd been there six years before.   **(I O)**
[78]   When I found the streets so wet, I naturally supposed it had been raining.   **(I U)**
[79]   The door-bell rang, but there was nobody there. That had already happened twenty times during the day.   **(S O)**
[80]   The place looked very different. They had been building everywhere.   **(S U)**

Activity continuing till then

[81]   I sold my house last summer. I had lived in it for twelve years, ever since my father died.   **(I O)**
[82]   By the time I arrived in Egypt, I had been studying Arabic for eighteen months.   **(I U)**
[83]   Till then, I had usually got up at seven; but . . .   **(S O)**

[84]   I had been getting up at six in order to work at the language,
         so I arrived rather tired.   (S U)

175   In this aspect we are dealing with a *prelude* to the past and
not merely with a sequence of past events. *In Caesar came,* (*then*) *he
saw,* (*then*) *he conquered* or in *First he kissed me, then he left me,*
SPPC moves forward with each event: one event may precede
another, but that is not the essential point in the pre-past. This
aspect is only adopted when the speaker has to make it clear, or
wishes to emphasise the fact, that some action preceded SPPC. Thus,
in example [81] *I had lived* is necessary to make it clear that the
speaker is referring to the period prior to the sale, which is the
SPPC; but where my father's death occurs in that order of events is
obvious without the particular distinction made by the Past Perfect
—hence *my father died.* Other examples:

[85]   The train left before I got to the station.

The order of events is clear. To emphasise it, I could say *the train
had left*; but it would be pedantic to mark *the train left* 'wrong'.

[86]   When I arrived at the station I found the train had left
         (two minutes before).

Here *had left* would be required to make it clear that the train's
departure on that occasion preceded my arrival, and especially to
mark the idea of such-and-such a time *before. I found the train left
two minutes before,* could mean that it usually left, or was scheduled
to leave, two minutes before the time I arrived.

[87]   'As the Chairman told you, I was in Ghana,' the lecturer
         began.

The speaker's being in Ghana preceded the Chairman's remarks.
However, not only is the order of events obvious to the audience,
but the speaker's primary concern is with his stay in Ghana, and it
is this that he is going to talk about.

[88]   I saw Michael on Sunday. He hadn't gone back to the office
         yet.

Here, *he hadn't gone back* is essential to the sense. *He didn't go back*
would suggest that his non-return was the consequence of my seeing
him; in any case, *yet* is only used in that sense with Present or Past
Perfect (see **160**). *He hasn't gone back* would mean *by now*; but
what the speaker meant was *by then.*

176   The Past Perfect can be a transfer to the pre-past of either the Present Perfect, as in [89] below or of the Past tense, as in [90]:

> [89]   A. The telegram has arrived.
>   B. Yes, you told me it had (arrived).
> [90]   A. It came last night.
>   B. Yes, you *told* me it came (*or* had come) last night.

The Past Perfect is obligatory when it is a transfer of the Present Perfect [89]; and then it is not associated with an adverbial of past time. When it is a transfer of the Past, as in [90], the Past Perfect is optional (provided the meaning is clear without it), and a past time adverbial is allowable.

The Post-present and the Future: Future Tenses

177   While the past is a chronicle of facts, of events that can be reported objectively, the future is a tale untold, a mirage of events unfulfilled. At its most certain, the future is the sphere of things we expect to happen. We *expect*, i.e. we look out into the future and imagine something happening. The problems of future tense in English involve not only aspects of activity and time, but also *moods*, i.e. the certainty, hesitation, willingness, determination, hope, sense of obligation or of prohibition, or pure neutrality, with which the speaker views what is to come. The unreal world ahead of us is not defined nearly so sharply as the period before now. There is no clear division between post-present and future comparable to the clear distinction between pre-present and past. What may or may not happen in the future is referred to in a variety of ways. Each expression of futurity is often complicated by subjective attitudes on the part of the speaker and his audience; but that will be discussed further in the next chapter. At present, we are concerned with aspects of activity and of time.

178   As the future is referred to in a variety of ways, we shall find no *one* Future tense. But the following might be called examples of 'Future tenses':

1. Mr Turner will leave tomorrow.
2. He is going to leave tomorrow. (See **152**.)
3. He is leaving tomorrow. (See **150**.)
4. He leaves tomorrow. (See **150**.)
5. He is to leave tomorrow.

He is to leave tomorrow is typical of the English of journalism. (In newspaper headlines, *is to leave* would be reduced to the infinitive, *to leave*.) This can be a simple statement of fact, or of plans that will lead to fulfilment. *Be to* is also used as a modal, implying a command, as we shall see in the next chapter.

179   There is plenty of evidence for choosing *will* + infinitive as the most generally used expression of futurity in modern English. *Shall* may be regarded as an optional replacement for *will* in association with *I* and *we*. That statement is based on wide observation of actual educted usage; and it is made despite the old prescriptive rule, summarised thus:

	Singular	*Plural*
1st Person	I shall	we shall
2nd Person	you will	you will
3rd Person	he, she, it will	they will

That 'rule' has been taught so often, and insisted on so severely, that it has undoubtedly had its effect on 'careful' writing. Yet, it is repeatedly broken, even by grammarians who teach it, as far as the use of *shall* is concerned. The prediction made by Kruisinga (in *A Handbook of Present-Day English* (1931–2)), that *shall* will ultimately disappear, has not yet come true, although *shan't* is rarely found in American English. As usage in this respect varies from region to region in the English-speaking world, and even from one individual speaker to another, there is no point in insisting on the prescriptive rule quoted above. Personally, I prefer to use *shall* with *I* and *we* on three occasions:

(*a*) when using *shall* with *I* or *we* would avoid a repetition of *will*, as in

[91]   The telephone will never ring and I shall never have to answer it;

(*b*) when I happen to feel that *I will* might sound more self-assertive than *I shall*; and

(*c*) when the repetition of the *w* sound in *we will* seems undesirable.

But I realise that others may feel differently about it. In any case, there are a great many occasions when I say neither *I will* nor *I shall*, but simply *I'll*. (I regard *I'll* as a weak form for *I will*; and *I shall* (pronounced /ʃəl/) as a weak form for *I shall* (/ʃæl/)).

180   I O, I U, S O and S U can be applied to the *will* Future tense, in exactly the same way as to the tenses we have discussed already. Thus:

[92] That's the phone. I'll answer it.   **I O**
[93] Good-bye. I'll see you on Wednesday.   **I O**
[94] Good-bye. I'll be thinking of you.   **I U**
[95] I'll be thinking of you tomorrow.   **I U**
[96] Don't worry. I'll write to you every day.   **S O**
[97] I'll be working late every day next week.   **S U**

181   Comparing examples [92] with [93], and [94] with [95], we can see that the Future tense with *will* can be used whether future time is specified or not. Contrast [92] with

[98] That's all right. I've answered it,

and [93] with

[99] Hallo again. I saw you on Wednesday, didn't I?

Nevertheless, we *can* make a distinction between post-present (our sixth aspect of time) illustrated like this:

Fig. 28

and the future, detached from point now (our seventh aspect) illustrated thus:

Fig. 29

We can make that distinction by using adverbials—*from now on* or the more formal *henceforth* for the post-present, and *tomorrow, next*

Friday etc. for the future. For example, compare example [92] with

[100] Don't touch the 'phone again. I'll answer it from now on.

182 Note *I'll be thinking of you.* [94] and [95] are examples of **I U**, and [97] of **S U**. All three are examples of progressive aspect, [94] applied to the post-present, [95] and [97] applied to the future detached from now. However, the same construction, *will be + -ing*, can have two other uses in which the speaker may not be thinking of the progressive at all. Consider this example:

[101] Mr Turner will be leaving on Thursday.

That may mean practically the same as *Mr T. is leaving on Thursday* (as in **150**); or it may be intended as a plain statement of future fact. The 'plain statement' avoids any tone of command on the part of the speaker, or any suggestion of determination on the part of Mr Turner—a feeling that might be conveyed by the words *Mr Turner will leave on Thursday:* see **216**. In fact, the use of the progressive in *will be leaving on Thursday* often suggests the avoidance of a too definite assertion that we saw in *I am hoping* etc. in **149**.

183 Although the distinction between post-present and future is not so clear as that between pre-present and past, it is possible to trace a different kind of distinction between *will* + infinitive and the other 'future tenses' given in **178**. Suppose we adopt the symbol T, standing for 'time of utterance' (as in **154**), and the symbol F, standing for 'future event'. Then I would say that, in *will* + infinitive, SPPC is at F, thus:

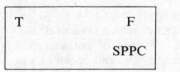

whereas with the other 'future tenses' SPPC is at T, with the speaker's attention directed towards F, thus:

This means that in saying *Mr T. will leave tomorrow*, the speaker's primary concern is with the future event; whereas with *Mr T. is*

going to leave, is leaving, leaves and is to leave, tomorrow, the speaker's primary concern is with the present factors—arrangements, plans, intentions, or whatever else they may be—that are expected to lead to Mr T.'s departure. Thus in saying

[102]   I'm going to call at the bank tomorrow and will pay the cheque in then.

my attention is first focused on T (my present intentions that will lead to F), then on F itself. However, the change from *I'm going to* (*call*) to *will* (*pay*) in [102] can also be accounted for (*a*) by an intuitive desire to avoid repeating the *-ing* form, and (*b*) by a shift from post-present to future, which is comparable with the shift from pre-present to past that we saw in **164**. It is noticeable that a text making a series of predictions, such as a weather forecast, may begin with *going to* and then be restricted to *will*, as in the following example:

[103]   Tomorrow is going to be colder everywhere. There will be snow on the hills; and motorists will find icy patches on many roads.

184   A choice between *will* and *be going to* often arises in ordinary spoken English: it is not likely to arise in formal written English, where *will* is usually preferred. When there *is* a choice, *be going to* is more appropriate when emphasis falls on present signs, intentions, preparations, etc., and *will* is more appropriate when such emphasis is absent or irrelevant. Note the presence or absence of the emphasis in the following examples:

[104]   (*The telephone rings.*) All right, I'll answer it.

The situation does not require the emphasis. *I'm going to answer it* would suggest a sequence of consideration, decision, action and ultimate fulfilment, by the end of which the caller would have lost patience and rung off.

[105]   I'm going to answer your letter, point by point.

Here the sequence of forethought, purpose, action and fulfilment is deliberately stressed.

[106]   I'll answer it if you give me time.

The conditions which might lead to future action are not provided.

[107]   I don't like this car. I'm going to sell it.

This breaks the news of my considered intentions and their possible consequence. Cp. *I think I'll sell it*, where the idea of intention is absent; or *I'll sell it for 400 pounds*, where emphasis is on the price.

[108] A. Tomorrow is going to be a busy day. (*So much has been planned, all the evidence points to it.*)
      B. Yes, it will be a busy day (*emphasis not repeated*).
[109] Tomorrow will be Tuesday.

Simple statement of future, with no justification for emphasis on T.

[110] I'm going to read your essay this evening and I'll discuss it with you tomorrow.

Emphasis on the first action, not repeated on the second.

[111] (I don't know the answer.) I'll know it next week.

In such a case, not only does emphasis fall on the point in future time, but the idea of purpose, action and fulfilment would be irrelevant with such an act of perception (see **147**). It would not be irrelevant in *find out*, as in *I don't know the answer but I'm going to find out*.

185 In temporal clauses (referring to time) and conditional clauses (beginning with *if*, *unless*, or a word of similar meaning), reference to the future is usually made in the Present tense, as in

[112] I'll come $\left\{\begin{array}{l}\text{when} \\ \text{as soon as}\end{array}\right\}$ I'm ready.
[113] We'll go out if it's fine.
[114] We'll stay indoors $\left\{\begin{array}{l}\text{until} \\ \text{unless}\end{array}\right\}$ it stops raining.

186 There are two complications in **185**. First, we must distinguish between a temporal clause, referring to time, as in

[115] Tell me when you're ready;

and a noun clause, object of a verb, as in

[116] Tell me when you'll be ready.

Example [115] means: You will be ready at some future time. At that time, let me know. Example [116] means: Tell me now what that future time will be.

187 Second, an *if*-clause referring to the future may contain an implied prediction, foretelling the future, as in

[117] If you are alone next Saturday night, 'phone me.

The implied prediction in that sentence is: You will be alone on

Saturday night. Note the tense in the *if*-clause of [117]. That example means: If the prediction comes true, 'phone me then.
Compare that with

[118]   If you will be alone on Saturday night, 'phone me.

That contains the same implied prediction: you will be alone on Saturday night. But [118] means: If that prediction can be safely made, telephone me now.

The Pre-future: Future Perfect

188   The eighth aspect of time, the prelude to the future, expressed by the Future Perfect, is comparable with the Present and Past Perfects. It could be illustrated as follows:

Fig. 30

The period which the speaker is now considering is imagined as being viewed from some future time, detached from now. The period may begin at any time before *then* (future), either in the pre-future or before the present moment. In other words, the period may or may not have begun at the time of speaking.

189   Examples:

[119]   I haven't answered that letter yet, but I'll have done so by Friday. (*On Friday I'll be able to look back and see that it has been answered.*)   (**I O**)

[120]   I started writing this book six months ago. By the end of this week I'll have written 200 pages.   (**I O**)

[121]   By then, I'll have been writing it for just over six months. (**I U**)

[122]   By the end of this year, the moon will have gone round the earth thirteen times.   (**S O**)

190 In example [119], *I'll do so by Friday* would also be acceptable, but it does not give the emphasis explained in parenthesis. In [122], *will go* would be acceptable, but only if that statement is made early in January. In [120] and [121], where the pre-future period begins before the time of speaking, then *I'll have written* and *I'll have been writing* are essential to the sense.

191 Note that, in the parenthesis in [119], I could have said *I'll be able to look back and see that it will have been answered*. But the use of the marked Future Perfect form, *will have been answered*, would make that sentence clumsy, so I used an unmarked form, *has been answered*, instead. Compare that with

[123] By the time I'm seventy, I shall have retired; and I'll get up late every morning *when I've retired*

and

[124] I'll let you have this book on Friday, if I've finished by then.

In other words, in temporal and conditional clauses the Future Perfect is normally replaced by the Perfect, just as the Future was replaced by the Present in [112], [113] and [114].

The Future as Seen from the Past: Future-in-the-Past

192 For this, the ninth aspect of time, the speaker's point of primary concern is in the past and his vision is directed forwards, to the more recent past, or to the present or even into the future:

Fig. 31

This aspect of time occurs to the speaker when he is reporting, from a viewpoint in the past, the kind of situation reflected in examples [92]–[97] **(180)**:

[125]   I said $\begin{cases} \text{I'd answer it.} \\ \text{I'd see you on Wednesday.} \\ \text{I'd be thinking of you.} \\ \text{etc.} \end{cases}$

Note the tenses used in the temporal and conditional clauses in

[126]   I said $\begin{cases} \text{I'd come when I was ready. (See [112].)} \\ \text{we'd go out if it was fine. ([113])} \\ \text{we'd stay indoors until it stopped raining. ([114])} \\ \text{I'd get up late when I'd retired.} \end{cases}$

The conversational *'d* in [125] and [126], before an infinitive (*come, see, be, go, stay, get*) would be replaced in formal written English by *would* (or optionally by *should* with *I* or *we*). Before a past participle (*retired* in [126]), *'d* is a weak form for *had*.

193   Since the future seen from the past extends beyond point now, as in Fig. 31, it would not be illogical, nor contrary to widespread usage, to say

[127]   I said $\begin{cases} \text{I'll answer it} \\ \text{I'll see you on Wednesday} \\ \text{we'll (or we'd) be thinking of you tomorrow} \end{cases}$

i.e. if the 'phone has not yet been answered, or if Wednesday or tomorrow have not yet come.

194   It is possible to express a continuation of the past comparable with the post-present (**177**). This is easily seen in

[128]   A. What were we doing (**I U**, *Past tense*) last lesson?
       B. You were telling us (**I U**, *Past tense*) about X, and then you were going to tell us (T $\longrightarrow$ F *transferred to the past*) about Y.

It is not so easily seen in

[129]   George dropped in yesterday evening just for a chat. We were dining at the Jones's, but he simply wouldn't go, so we were terribly late.

There, *we were dining* is a past equivalent of *we are dining* (Future tense No. 3, in **178**), and means 'we had arranged to dine'. Similarly, *We sailed at three* is a past equivalent of Future tense No. 4 in

[130]   We really couldn't lunch with you on our last day. We sailed at three and had so much to do before we left.

There, *We sailed at three* = We were due to sail then.

THE TENSES

195 The tenses are thus verbal forms and constructions which express aspects of activity combined with aspects of time. As examples, the tenses of the verb *ask*, in the active voice, are set out below, with the names that are now commonly attached to them:

Aspect of time	Aspect of activity	Example	Tense
1. Unlimited ⎫ and ⎬ 2. Present ⎭	O	I ask	Simple Present
	U	I am asking	Present Progressive
3. Pre-present	O	I have asked	Present Perfect
	U	I have been asking	Present Perfect Progressive
4. Past	O	I asked	Simple Past
	U	I was asking	Past Progressive
5. Pre-past	O	I had asked	Past Perfect
	U	I had been asking	Past Perfect Progressive
6. Post-present ⎫ and ⎬ 7. Future ⎭	O	I will ask	Simple Future
	U	I will be asking	Future Progressive
8. Pre-future		I will have asked	Future Perfect
		I will have been asking	Future Perfect Progressive
9. Future seen from the past	O	I would ask	Future-in-the-Past
	U	I would be asking	

Tenses in the passive voices would fit into a similar scheme:

1 and 2	I am asked
3	I have been asked
4	I was asked
5	I had been asked
6 and 7	I will be asked
8	I will have been asked
9	I would be asked

To the above, we must add *I used to ask*, *I used to be asked*, which can be regarded as a Past tense referring to habitual action no longer performed; and the other 'Future tenses' set out in **178**.

Special Uses of the Tenses

196   *The Simple Present* is customarily used

(*a*) as the 'historic present' to make a narrative of past events seem more dramatic, and especially in a synopsis of a novel or play. Each new step in the story is related in the Simple Present, while the Present Progressive serves as a background against which action takes place:

[131]   The villagers are quietly going about their daily tasks when a stranger rides up and startles them all by firing his pistol into the air.

(*b*) in newspaper headlines reporting the latest news. Note that the detailed report beneath the headlines would relate past events in the Past tense;

(*c*) in captions accompanying a picture illustrating past action, as in

[132]   Aeneas carries his father out of burning Troy.

197   *The Present Progressive* may be used

to refer to action in progress immediately before the time of utterance, as in B's response:

[133]   A. I've just seen a lion in the garden.
        B. A lion? What *are* you talking about?

198   Depending on the context in which it is used, the *Present Perfect Progressive* can stress

(*a*) incompletion in contrast to completion:

[134]   I've been reading your book (*incompletion*), and have already read the first three chapters (*completion*).

(*b*) a temporary state of affairs, as in

[135]   We've been living in a hotel so far, but soon we hope to move into a furnished flat.

(*c*) irritation at somebody else's action:

[136]   Who's been using my tape-recorder?

199   (*a*) The *Simple Past* is used to refer to an act which is desirable or even obligatory but which has not yet been fulfilled:

[137]   Hurry up! It's time we left.

(*b*) It may also be used when the speaker is making a request or giving an invitation without assuming that his audience will agree:

[138]   I wondered (*meaning* I wonder now) whether you could lend me your typewriter.

(*c*) For the use of the past tense in *if*-clauses and after *wish*, see **204** and **205**.

200   The *Past Progressive* may be used

(*a*) to refer to past intentions, cancelled or otherwise unfulfilled. Whereas the dictator might declare *I cross the Rubicon tomorrow*, and the ordinary mortal say *I'm crossing it tomorrow*, an undecided man might play the role of B in the following dialogue:

[139]   A. What are you doing tomorrow?
        B. Well—er—I was crossing the Rubicon—but now—er. . . .

i.e. I was thinking of crossing it before you asked me, but now I am willing to do whatever you suggest.

(*b*) similarly, in a hesitant request or invitation, as in [138]:

[140]   I was wondering whether . . .

(*c*) to refer to action that ought to be in progress but has not yet started, as in [137]:

[141]   Hurry up! It's time we were leaving.

Note once more how the Progressive form is used to express a less definite attitude than the non-progressive form.

201   For the use of the Past Perfect in *if*-clauses and after *wish*, see **204** and **205**.

Sequence of Tenses

202   The question of which combination of tenses should be used in English in a piece of consecutive speech or writing is primarily a matter of deciding which tense is suitable for each separate action; and that, as we have seen earlier in this chapter, depends on the aspect of activity and the aspect of time with which the speaker is concerned, and on whether a marked or unmarked form is required. Take care of each tense, therefore, and the sequence will usually take care of itself. However, since sudden and too frequent changes of point of primary concern are undesirable unless deliberately intended, and can be confusing to the reader, Present tenses tend to be found with Present, Present Perfect and Future, while Past tenses tend to be found with Past, Past Perfect and Future-in-the-Past. In addition, there are four areas of particular difficulty as far as tense sequence is concerned. They are dealt with in the following paragraphs.

203   Firstly, for the tenses used in sentences with conditional and temporal clauses having future reference, look back at examples [112]–[118], and [123]–[124].

204   Secondly, for the tenses used in *if*-sentences generally, we must consider whether the *if*-clause assumes something to be a fact, or whether it imagines a non-fact to be actual fact. Thus:

Assuming a fact

(*a*) If you tell the truth, people trust you.

(*b*) If you are telling the truth, we have no time to lose.

(*c*) If you have studied all this book, you know a lot.

(*d*) If you have been walking in this heat, you must be very thirsty.

(*e*) If we told Father the truth, he never punished us.

(*f*) If you were walking all day yesterday, no wonder you are tired today.

(*g*) If you had met John before, why didn't you speak to him last night?

(*h*) If you had been swimming before breakfast yesterday, no wonder you ate such a lot.

(*i*) If you tell the truth tomorrow, you will be quite safe.

(*j*) If you are playing tennis next Saturday, we shall not be able to go for our usual walk.

(*k*) If you have read this report by next Friday, you will be able to discuss it at our meeting on Friday afternoon.

(*l*) Didn't I say that if you told the truth you would be quite safe?

Imagining non-fact to be actual fact

(*m*) (You never tell the truth.) If you told the truth, people would trust you.

(*n*) (You're not telling the truth.) If you were telling the truth, you would be looking me straight in the eye.

(*o*) (You have not told the truth.) If you had told the truth, you wouldn't have blushed like that.

(*p*) (You did not tell the truth.) If you had told the truth, you would not have been punished.

(*q*) (You had not met John before I introduced him to you.) If you had met him before, I am sure he would have recognised you.

(*r*) (We shall not go out in this rain.) If we went out, we should only get soaking wet. *Or* If we were to go out, etc.

(*s*) (We shall not be playing tennis tomorrow.) If we were playing tennis, we shouldn't be able to finish our work.

205 Thirdly, note the tenses used with *wish*, which also imagines non-fact to be actual fact:

(*a*) I'm not enjoying myself: I wish I was (*or* were).

(*b*) I'm working today: I wish I wasn't (*or* weren't).

(*c*) I can't swim: I wish I could.

(*d*) I don't feel well: I wish I felt better.

(*e*) I feel tired: I wish I didn't.

(*f*) I did not see that film: I wish I had seen it.

(*g*) I'll lend you my camera: I wish you would.

206 Finally, note the tenses commonly used in reporting speech in the past:

Direct speech	*Indirect speech*
(*a*) 'The shop's shut.'	He said the shop was shut.
(*b*) 'The men have gone.'	He said the men had gone.
(*c*) 'They went at 5 o'clock.'	He said they went (*or* had gone) at five o'clock.
(*d*) 'Someone will come.'	He said someone would come.
(*e*) 'I shall come.'	He said he would come.

Indirect speech can have the Past Perfect in both (*b*) and (*c*). However, while the Past Perfect is obligatory in (*b*), it is optional in (*c*): see **176**. In (*e*), *shall* is optional with *I* or *we* (see **179**), but only *will* or *would* occurs in plain future, or future-in-the-past, with *you* or *he*. *Can* and *may* in direct speech become *could* and *might* in indirect; but the *should* of obligation, and *must* and *ought to*, in direct speech remain unchanged when speech is reported as past. However, the changes of tenses in the dependent clause, though usual, are not obligatory if the reported fact is still valid, so that *He said the shop is shut, He said he will come* are quite acceptable if, when those statements are made, the shop still *is* shut, he still *will* come, and so on. See also **192**; and for further comment on direct and indirect speech, see Chapter 12, paragraph **388**.

CHAPTER 6

Auxiliary and Modal Verbs

207

	Auxiliaries		Modals	
	A	B	C	D
(a)	am('m)	—	(f) will('ll)	won't
	is('s)	isn't	shall	shan't
	are('re)	aren't	would('d)	wouldn't
	was	wasn't	should	shouldn't
	were	weren't		
(b)	have('ve)	haven't	(g) can	can't
	has('s)	hasn't	could	couldn't
	had('d)	hadn't	may	—
			might	mightn't
(c)	do	don't		
	does	doesn't	must	mustn't
	did	didn't	ought	oughtn't
(d)	will('ll)	won't	(h) need	needn't
	shall	shan't	dare	daren't
	would('d)	wouldn't		
	should	shouldn't		
(e)	used	?		

208 What are here called auxiliaries include:

(a) parts of the verb *be* (*am, is, are, was, were*) which are used with *-ing* to form the progressive (*I am working*) or with *-ed* to form the passive (*I am asked*);

(b) parts of the verb *have* (*have, has, had*) used to form the perfective (*have worked, have been working, had worked* etc.);

(c) parts of the verb *do*, used to form the interrogative and the negative of the Simple Present and the Simple Past;

(*d*) *will* and *shall* which, with the bare infinitive, form the principal Future tense; and *would* and *should* which form a Future-in-the-Past, at least in indirect speech;

(*e*) *used* + *to*-infinitive referring to a past state of affairs no longer prevailing (**172**).

209 What are here called the modals also include

(*f*) *will, shall, would* and *should*; they include
(*g*) *can, could, may, might, must* and *ought*; and
(*h*) *need* and *dare*, which may be used as modals or as 'full verbs'.
The functions of the modals will be the main theme of this chapter.

210 The auxiliaries and the modals listed in columns A and C in **207** have one important syntactic feature in common: they act as 'operators' in the following six operations:

1. Followed immediately by *not*, they make the verbal part of a sentence negative, as in

[1] We have not finished breakfast yet.

The reduced forms are usual in fluent, unemphasised, everyday speech. Thus *we have* or *we have not* before *finished* would be typical of formal writing and deliberate speech; *we've, we've not* or *we haven't* before *finished* would be typical of normal speech and informal writing. Note that in Columns B and D, operator + *n't* is written as one word.

2. *Operator* + *subject* + *rest of the verb* provides the interrogative form:

[2] Have you finished breakfast yet?

Examples [2] and [3] below are of questions requiring the answer Yes or No. For questions beginning with *what, who* etc. see **376**.

3. Operator + *n't* + subject + rest of the verb provides the negative-interrogative form:

[3] Haven't you finished breakfast yet?

Have you not finished? would be either more formal or more deliberate. More formal still would be a construction like *Have not instructions been published?* (which is unusual when the subject is a personal pronoun).

4. The operators supply the verbal past of *tag* questions:

[4] You've finished, haven't you?
     You haven't finished, have you?

The operator and its tense in the tag must be the same as those in the main part of the sentence.

5.   The operators supply an emphatic affirmative, as in

[5]   A. I interrupted you. You haven't finished.
       B. That's all right. I have finished (have *stressed*).

6.   They act as a substitute for the whole of the predicate, avoiding repetition, as in

[6]   George hasn't finished breakfast, but we have (*i.e. we have finished breakfast*).

211   In the active voice, the Simple Present and the Simple Past contain no operator; and *do, does, did* supply this lack for the six operations in **210**. The main verb is then in the bare infinitive (without *to*) whatever the subject and tense may be. Thus:

1.   [7]   He likes coffee but he doesn't like tea.
2.   [8]   Does he take sugar? Did he always take it?
3.   [9]   Don't you like it? Doesn't he? Didn't he like it?
4.   [10]   You like milk, don't you?
              You didn't always like it, did you?
5.   [11]   A. You don't like cream, do you?
              B. Oh, but I *do* like it (do *stressed*).
6.   [12]   I think you made the right choice. In fact, we all do
              (*i.e. think you made the right choice*).

Do is also used to form the negative-interrogative (e.g. *Do not speak to the driver. Don't move*) as well as an emphatic form of the imperative (*Do be quiet*).

212   All the auxiliaries and modals in **207** can be used in those six ways, except at the following points:

(*a*) The reduced forms in columns A and C ('*m*, '*ll*, etc.) will not occur at the very beginning or very end of a sentence or clause. Thus:

[13]   A. I think it's beginning to snow?
        B. Is it? Why, so it is.

(*b*) There is no alternative negative form to *I'm not*; but *Aren't I?* can informally replace *Am I not?*

(*c*) *Used*, which requires the *to*-infinitive, fits easily into operation 5; but in the other cases there is popular pressure against such forms as *Use(d)n't you to (do that)?*, as well as uncertainty about how *use(d)n't* should be spelt. On the other hand, the widely heard **didn't use(d) to, Did you use(d) to? Didn't you use(d) to?* have not gained complete respectability. The following would, I consider, be acceptable ways of overcoming these difficulties:

1. Now I type my letters but *I used not to* (or *usedn't to*).
2. & 3. Did(n't) you (usually) type them?
4. You used to type them, didn't you?
5. I don't type my letters now, but I used to (*used* stressed).
6. I used to write everything by hand, and so did my brother (*i.e.* he used to write everything by hand too).

(*d*) *Ought*, also followed by the *to*-infinitive, presents similar problems. There is some popular reluctance to say *ought not to*, but **didn't ought to* is generally regarded as sub-standard. Any uncertainty about using *ought* can usually be overcome by replacing it by *should*. The following would therefore be acceptable:

1. You ought not to (*or* oughtn't to) say that.
2. What ought we to do now?
3. Oughtn't we to leave? *Or more formal* Ought we not to?
4. We ought to go now, oughtn't (*or* shouldn't) we?
5. I haven't read that book, but I know I *ought* to (ought *stressed*).
6. Yes, you ought to read it, and so should I.

(*e*) *Cannot* is normally spelt as one word. But there is a difference between *You cannot stay here*, where *can* is negated, and *You can not stay if you prefer to leave*, where *stay* is negated. A similar comment would apply to the other modals. *You could not* (*or couldn't*) *stay* negates *could*, whereas *You could not stay* (*not* stressed, and separated from *could*) negates *stay*.

(*f*) *Mayn't* is excluded from **207** as old-fashioned.

(*g*) *Need* and *dare* only occur as modals before a bare infinitive and with negative or interrogative meanings. As 'full verbs', they could be used in all the six operations with the help of *do*:

Modal	*Full verb*
1. I need/dare not go	You don't need/dare to go.
2. Need/Dare we go?	Do we need/dare to go?
3. ———	Don't you need/dare to go?
4. We needn't/daren't go yet, need/dare we?	We don't need/dare to go yet, do we?
5. ———	You say I don't need/dare to go, but I do (*do* stressed).
6. ———	John needs to read this again and so do I.

In the Modal column, 3 is unfilled since *Needn't we go?* implies an affirmative. On the other hand, *I hardly/scarcely need tell you* would be acceptable, as semi-negatives.

The Modals

213   *Will* can be a purely temporary auxiliary, foretelling the future. At the same time, it can be a modal expressing some personal attitude towards an unfulfilled event. *Will/shall* + infinitive therefore belong both to a time system and to a modal system, thus:

Fig. 32

214   All the modals, except *shall*, have two main functions, which we may call primary and secondary. In their primary function, they express some degree of freedom, or lack of freedom, to act—from complete liberty to inescapable prohibition; and this freedom, or lack of it, can apply to the speaker, or to the person(s) he is addressing, or to some person(s) to whom he is referring.

215   In their secondary function, all except *shall* act as one of the devices English has for allowing the speaker to give his evaluation of the truth of the statement he is making. (Other devices include the use of *seem* and verbs of similar meaning, as in *It seems to be raining over there*, and 'disjunct' adverbials (see **355**), as in *Apparently, we had a lot of rain last night*.) We shall see the difference between these two functions as we examine each of the modals in turn.

Will

216   In its primary function, *will* can express certainty, or volition, or a combination of both—certainty that nothing can stop the event from taking place, or the will to ensure that it is accomplished. The speaker's own certainty and/or volition could be an important feature in

[14]   We will find a cure for cancer;
[15]   He will do what I tell him;

and

[16]   Let our motto be: I will not be afraid.

The will of the person addressed is referred to in

[17]   A. May I help you?
       B. Yes, if you will.

A third person's volition is suggested in

[18]   Mr Turner will see you soon. He won't keep you long.
[19]   Some people *will* leave this door open (will *strongly stressed and indicating persistent habit*). They *won't* close it properly.
[20]   That old man will sit there for hours looking out to sea. (*He has done it so often before that one can safely predict that it will happen again and again.*)

217   How much volition is expressed by *will* depends on many factors, including the speaker's own intentions, the context of the utterance, the animateness or inanimateness of the subject, the degree to which the action is subject to human control. There is no volition, but there may be certainty, in *The rain will come soon*: there may be volition as well as certainty in *Mr Turner will come soon*. There may be no volition in *We'll know the results tomorrow*, but plenty of it in *We'll find out the results now*.

218   The modal *will* is commonly used in questions

[21]   Will you have some tea? (What are your wishes?)
[22]   Won't you have some more? (What are your wishes?)
[23]   Will you post this letter for me? (Those are my wishes: I hope you are willing to carry them out.)
[24]   Will you sit down! (That is my wish and command.)

Note that [21], [22] and [23] would be spoken with a rising intonation, but [24] with a sharply falling one.

219   There is no restriction on the use of the modal *will* in *if*-clauses: see **185**. Thus:

[25]   If you will smoke, please go outside.
[26]   If you will sit down for a moment I will see if Mr Turner is in.

220   In its secondary function, *will* allows the speaker to make a statement, not asserting that it is true but suggesting that it will prove to be so. *I suppose* or *I expect* can usually, and often is, added to the statement:

[27]   (The 'phone rings.) That will be Jeremy, I expect.
[28]   I wonder where the boys are. They'll be coming home from school now, I suppose.

Will Have-ed

221   Besides expressing the Future Perfect, *will have-ed* can indicate a present supposition about the pre-present or past, as in

[29]   You will all have heard the news last night.

That means *I suppose that you heard*. . . . Without the adverbial of past time, *last night*, it could also mean *I suppose that you have heard*. . . .

Would

222   (*a*) *Would* has a temporal function, and serves as a Future-in-the-Past, in past reported speech (*I told you it would rain*: see **192**). It rarely serves this purpose in an independent clause, though it can do so in the course of a narrative, as in

[30]   The climbers had reached 5,000 metres. Soon they would see the summit.

(*b*) In conditional sentences, whereas the Present tense in the *if*-clause commonly accompanies *will* in the main clause, the Past tense in the *if*-clause attracts *would* in the main.

[31]   If you heated this liquid, it would explode (**204** (*m*)).

That is an example of what is called the Conditional *would*.

(*c*) *Would* can also act as the past equivalent of the modal *will* in past reported speech. Thus example [14] could become

[14a]   I told you we would find a cure . . .

and a similar comment would apply to examples [15]–[24] inclusive. Thus:

[23a]   I asked you if you would post this letter. . . .

Exercises requiring students to 'put *will* into the past tense' are often meaningless (unless past reported speech is intended). *Will you have some tea?* is an utterance that only makes sense if it applies to present time, and it is not made past by converting *Will* into *Would*. A similar remark applies to all the examples [14]–[18] inclusive, and to [21]–[24] inclusive. However, [19] and [20] can be 'put into the past tense', in the following way:

[19a] Some people *would* leave this door open. They *wouldn't* close it properly. So now we keep it locked.

[20a] The old man would sit there for hours. . . .

Example [20a] is typical of narrative style.

223 *Would you have some tea?* (cp. **218**) is an illustration of *would* as a separate modal, expressing meanings that are similar to those of the modal *will*, but more hesitantly, and with greater deference to the audience. The same applies to examples [22]–[24], where the speaker also has a choice between *will* and *would*. But *will* could not replace *would* in

[32] Would you like some tea, or would you prefer coffee?

nor

[33] Would you mind posting this letter for me?

224 The modal *would* occurs freely in *if*-clauses (cp. **219**). Thus:

[34] If you would take a seat for a moment, I'll see if Mr Turner is in.

Would there suggests willingness on your part. It makes a hesitant suggestion in

[35] If you would be interested, I'll send you a copy.

225 A special idiomatic use of *would* is found in an example like:

[36] A. I've lost my ticket.
B. You *would* (do a thing like that) (would *stressed*),

meaning 'that is characteristic of you'.

Would or Should

226 *Should* can, optionally, replace *would* with *I* and *we* (cp. **192**) in the Future-in-the-Past and Conditional uses. But this replacement could cause ambiguity: *should* in *I told you we should find a cure* . . . might be mistaken for the *should* of obligation (see **234**).

Note:

[37]   I should be grateful if you would reply urgently,

which takes advantage of the option of using *should* with *I* or *we* and avoids the repetition of *would*. Replacement of *would* by *should* is unacceptable when *would* is a modal in its own right, as in

[38]   I was never good at football. I would miss the ball completely.

[39]   I would willingly help you, if I were free.

227   *Would* has a secondary modal function, allowing the speaker to make a statement but with less certainty than in **220**:

[27a]   (The 'phone rings.) That would be Jeremy, probably.

[28a]   The boys would be coming home from school, I imagine.

Would Have-ed

228   (*a*) *Would have-ed* can be a transfer of the Future Perfect to the past, so that *I'll have finished that by Friday* can become *I told you I'd have finished.* . . .

(*b*) It can be a transfer of the Conditional *would* to the past, so that *If I met him again, I would recognise him* can become *If I had met him again, I would have recognised him.*

(*c*) It can also be a present, hesitant assumption about past action, *would* serving the secondary modal function, as in

[27a]   A. Someone telephoned you last night.
        B. That would have been Jeremy, I would say.

Shall

229   *Shall*, like *will* (**213**) can be a purely temporary auxiliary, optionally replacing *will* with *I* and *we*. Even in its temporal use, however, there may be a private colouring (see **179**). Personally, I use *will* as a weak unmarked form, a neutral indicator of the future, or as a strong unmarked form combining prediction with certainty; and I use *shall* as a marked form, expressing modesty (I hope) towards my audience and readers. This already suggests that I use *shall* as a modal, in the sense of paragraph **213**. I realise that, with other speakers and writers, the decision to use *shall* instead of *will* with *I* or *we* may be a matter of taste, habit or chance.

230   *Shall* is certainly a modal, expressing the speaker's deference to the wishes of his audience, in

[40]   Shall I open the window (*i.e. would you like me to do that?*)
[41]   Shall we go, or do you want to stay longer?
[42]   Shall the waiter serve coffee now?

[42] is perhaps rarer than [40] and [41], and would often be replaced by *Do you want* (or *Would you like*) *the waiter to serve. . .?*)

231   *Shall*, as a modal is also a mark of decision or determination on the part of the speaker(s) with regard to the actions of others, as in

[43]   There shall be no more wars

—a wise decree, deciding that everyone must henceforth live in peace, but not an assurance that war will never occur again.

[44]   The enemy shall not pass. (We are determined not to let them.)
[45]   Every member shall pay his annual subscription within the first fortnight of the year.

—a decision affecting every member of a certain organisation, but not an assurance that every member will pay his subscription promptly.

[46]   You shall have whatever you want, I promise you.

Shall Have-ed

232   *Shall have-ed* expresses Future Perfect and is available, optionally, with *I* and *we*.

Should

233   (*a*) *I shall be late* can become *I told you I should be late* in indirect speech.

(*b*) Also in indirect speech, examples [40]–[42] would become *I asked if I should open . . . , if we should go . . . , if the waiter should serve coffee now*. [44] would become *We were determined the enemy should not pass*; and [46], *I promised you should have whatever you wanted*.

234   In its primary function, the modal *should* suggests an obligation (that is escapable) or action that is advisable.

[47] Applications should be submitted by March 31st at the latest. (*Quotation from an official document.*)

[48] You should take more exercise. (*That is advisable.*)

[49] I should take more exercise, if I were you.

In [49] the speaker tactfully lays the obligation on himself, though it is intended for the person addressed.

235 *Should* also makes a supposition. In

[50] If you should be interested, I'll send you a copy,

the speaker is more hesitant in supposing that you are interested than in example [35] (*If you would be interested. . . .*). He is still more hesitant in

[51] Should you be interested (by any chance). . . .

where *should* is usually strongly stressed and is not replaceable by *would*.

236 The 'suggestive' or 'putative' use of *should* also occurs in

[52] I'm surprised that you should feel so upset,

Should could be omitted from [52], in which case my surprise would have been caused by the *fact* that you are upset. The use of *should* in [52] suggests that I am surprised by the *idea* of your being upset now. In

[53] It is right that we should tell him the truth,

should, referring to future action, cannot be omitted. Notice the difference between

[54] I propose that Mr Turner should be or should act as Chairman,

where *should* could be omitted, with *be* and *act* as subjunctive, and

[55] I believe that he should be Chairman,

where *should* cannot be left out. [54] makes a proposal about the future, while [55] only states what course of action somebody considers desirable. *Should* remains unchanged if [54] and [55] are reported in the past, e.g.

[56] I proposed/believed that he should be Chairman.

237 Note the special use of *should* in

[57] I can't understand why you should say that (*i.e. I can't understand what makes you say it now*).

238 In its secondary function, *should* is a device by which the speaker can indicate that he supposes the statement he is making to be true:

[58] According to the map, this should be our way (*i.e. looking at the map, I think this is our way*).

Should Have-ed

239 *Should have-ed* can (*a*) optionally replace *would have-ed* in **228** (*a*) with *I* and *we*, and

(*b*) refer to past obligation unfulfilled. Compare example [47] with

[59] Your application is too late. You should have submitted it by March 31st.

Similarly, *should not have-ed* refers to action taken in the past despite obligation not to take it, as in *You should not have left it till it was too late*.

(*c*) *Should have-ed* would refer to the past in

[52a] I'm surprised that you should have felt upset (*i.e. I'm surprised at the idea of your being upset then*).

Similarly,

[57a] I can't understand why you should have said that

means I can't understand what made you say it.

(*d*) As with the other modals, in the secondary function *should have-ed* marks a present supposition about the past. Thus:

[58a] We took the wrong road an hour ago. According to the map, the road going east should have been our way.

Ought

240 *Ought to* and *should* are often inter-replaceable (see **212** (*d*)), but only in the sense of obligation. Thus [48] could be re-worded:

[48a] You ought to take more exercise.

But *ought to* would not be acceptable instead of *should* in [49]. To some speakers, *ought to* suggests an obligation the fulfilment of which is overdue or may be delayed. In the official statement in [47], if *should* were replaced by *ought to*, readers might suppose that it would not matter if applications were submitted after the date mentioned. A clerk receiving an enquiry about applications on, say, March 30th, could rightly say

[59a]   You'll have to make up your mind quickly. Applications ought to be in by tomorrow, and I doubt whether yours will arrive in time.

241   *Ought to* could not replace *should*, in any of the examples in **233**, **235** and **237**. In **236**, the only example in which *ought to* could replace *should* is [55], which was only included in that paragraph as a contrast with [54].

242   In its secondary function, *ought to* has a meaning equivalent to that of *should* in **238**.

Ought to Have-ed

243   (*a*) *Ought to have-ed* refers to past obligation unfulfilled, and could replace *should have-ed* in example [59]. Similarly, *ought not to have-ed* refers to action taken despite obligation not to take it.

(*b*) In the secondary function, *ought to have-ed* could replace *should have-ed*, as in [58a].

Must, Have To, Be To

244   *Must* differs from *should* and *ought to* in that it indicates obligation that is considered inescapable: *We must be free, or die*, as Wordsworth put it.

The past equivalent of *must* is *had to*, though *must* can remain in past reported speech:

[60]   'I must be very frank with you',

refers to the present, while

[60a]   I had to be very frank with him

refers to the past. [60] could also refer to the future, though *I'll have to be very frank with him* makes the future reference clearer. [60] in past reported speech could either be *I told him I must be very frank . . .* or *I told him I had to be. . . .* The latter would make it clear that the obligation belonged to the past.

245   There are two ways of negating *must* + infinitive: we can express an absence of obligation, by saying, e.g. *You need not*, or

You do not have to, *go*; or we can negate what follows *must*, and say, for example, Y*ou must not go*: Thus:

You need not go=You are *not required* to go.
You must not go=You are required *not to go*.

246 *Have to* (do something), or, informally, *have got to* (do it) suggests that the obligation is prescribed by some authority, regulation, or by unavoidable circumstances. *Have to* is not included as a modal as defined in **210**, since *have* in this construction can be used as a 'full verb', with the complete range of inflections and tenses that would be found with, e.g. *ask*, as in **195**: see **248**.

247 *I am to* (*do something*) means that I am obliged to do it by a plan, agreement, time-table or instruction, or something similar, which I am not free to ignore. Note that the journalistic

[61]   Henderson is to stay as Finance Minister,

which simply makes a statement about the future, a statement based on known plans, while

[61a]   You are to stay here. You are not to leave this room,

are firm commands.

248 The following table shows how the idea of *obligation without the option of avoiding it* is expressed in the various tenses, and how *have to* can compensate for the defectiveness of *must*:

Tense	*Affirmative*	*Opposite*	*Negative*
Present	(i) I am obliged to (go)	am forbidden to	am not obliged to
	(ii) I must (go)	must not	need not
	(iii) I have to (go)	—(1)	do not have to
	(iv) I am to (go)	am not to	—
Pre-Present	(i) I have been obliged to	have been forbidden to	have not been obliged to
	(ii) —	—	—
	(iii) have had to	—	have not had to
Past	(i) I was obliged to	was forbidden to	was not obliged to
	(ii) must (**244**)	must not	did not need to
	(iii) had to	—	did not have to
	(iv) was to(2)	was not to	—

Pre-Past	(i)	had been obliged to	had been forbidden to	had not been obliged to
	(ii)	—	—	—
	(iii)	had had to	—	had not had to
	(iv)	was to have (gone)(3)	—	—
Future	(i)	will be obliged to	will be forbidden to	will not be obliged to
	(ii)	must	must not	need not/will not need to
	(iii)	will have to	—	will not have to
	(iv)	am to	am not to	—

Notes 1. A blank in the table indicates that the corresponding form is not used in that position. 2. *I was to go to London*=that was the plan, those were my instructions. 3. *I was to have gone*= It had been planned that I should go, but I had not gone.

249 In its secondary function, *must*[1] suggests that the truth of the speaker's statement is inescapable:

[62]   This *must* be the way, surely:

there the speaker feels no doubt about it. Note that the contrary to [62] would be

[63]   This *can't* be the way, surely.

Must Have-ed

250 This construction is used only in the secondary function of *must*, so that

[64]   You must have been tired

means *I'm sure you were tired*, while

[65]   You can't have gone to the right house

means *I'm sure you did not.* . . .

Can

251 *You can go* means that you have complete freedom to act,

[1] Under American and television influence, there is a growing (perhaps temporary) tendency to replace *You must be joking* by *You've got to be joking*. This is not, I feel, typical of standard British English.

whether that freedom depends on (*a*) your own ability; (*b*) lack of opposition; (*c*) positive permission; or (*d*) what circumstances allow.

[66] You can drive my car

may refer to your present ability or to the permission given to you by the speaker. But

[67] You can drive my car perfectly

refers only to your ability. Example [66] could refer to future (as well as present) but only with the meaning of permission, not ability. To express future ability, one would have to say e.g.

[68] You'll be able to drive it perfectly after a few more lessons.

However, in an *if*-clause we can use *can* to refer to future ability:

[69] If you can use this typewriter properly in a month's time, you may keep it.

Freedom from other engagements is suggested in

[70] I can see you tomorrow, at 10 o'clock,

though *I'll be able to see you* marks the future reference more strongly.

252 *Can* frequently precedes verbs of perception, e.g. *I can see a ship. Can you hear me? I can remember exactly what happened.* In such examples, the meaning is almost identical with that of *I see. Do you hear? I remember.* However, in *I can see* etc. we are more concerned with the freedom to perceive, rather than with the result. This appears clearly in the past: *We had a marvellous view from the top—we could see for miles*; but *Have you seen my watch anywhere? Yes, I saw it on your dressing-table.*

253 *Can*, in a question, can ask permission, as in

[71] Can I borrow your pen, please?

To that, the answer could be *Yes of course you can* (permission granted, as in one interpretation of example [66]), or *No, I'm afraid you can't.*

254 In its secondary function, *can* suggests that it is perfectly possible that the statement the speaker is making is true:

[72] This can be the answer, I think.

In this sense, *can* often begins a question, as in *Can this be right?*

Can Have-ed

255   An example of the secondary function of *can*, making a present assumption about the past or pre-past, would be

[73]   He can have been delayed

meaning *I think it is possible he was, or has been, delayed.*

Could

256   (*a*) *Can* becomes *could* when in past reported speech, e.g.

[66a]   You said I could drive your car.
[71a]   I asked if I could borrow your pen.

(*b*) *Could* refers to past ability, as in

[74]   I could drive perfectly ten years ago.

We can interpret [74] as meaning not only that I had the ability but also that I succeeded in driving perfectly on many occasions. *We could see Mont Blanc clearly* implies that we actually saw it. But when we are referring to a single accomplishment subject to human control, *could* refers only to ability, not to the accomplishment itself. Thus:

[75]   I could pass my driving test

does not mean that I actually passed it. Accomplishment in that case could be expressed by *I was able*, or *I managed to pass it* or *I succeeded in passing it* or, simply, *I passed it*. On the other hand, *I could not pass my test* means that I lacked the ability, and therefore failed.

257   (*a*) *Could* refers to possible freedom from other engagements in

[70a]   I could see you tomorrow at 10, perhaps,

which is less definite than *I can see you* . . . ([70]).
(*b*) *Could* also asks for, and grants, permission, as in

[71b]   Could I borrow your pen, please?

to which the answer might be *Yes of course you could* or *No I'm afraid you couldn't.* There, *could* is more hesitant, less direct, than *can.*

258   In its secondary function, *could* serves a similar purpose to that of *can* in **254**, but suggests some doubt as well as possibility. Thus:

[76]   This could be the answer. What do you think?

Like *can* in this sense, *could* often begins a question, e.g. *Could this be right?*

Could Have-ed

259   (*a*) This expresses past ability unused, or past permission of which advantage was not, or has not been, taken:

[77]   A. Did you get to the top (of the mountain)?
       B. We could have done, but we didn't try.
[78]   Why did you walk? You could have taken my car.
       I said you could use it.

(*b*) [76a]   That could have been the answer (see [76])

means 'I assume now that that answer was probably right, though I am still doubtful about it.'
(*c*) Note the example

[79]   When I saw the results I could have wept,

meaning I felt like weeping (but did not).

Be Able To

260   Just as *have to* can compensate for the defectiveness of *must* (**248**), so *be able to* and *be unable to* can compensate for the defectiveness of *can*. Thus to express the idea of *can* in the *infinitive*, *present participle*, and *present perfect*, we can say:

[80]   Candidates must be able to speak English fluently.
[81]   Being able to speak both languages, you must act as interpreter.
[82]   We have been unable to trace your reply to our letter of 17th November.

We are unable to is often preferred in formal English to the more abrupt *cannot* and the still more abrupt *can't*.

May

261   (*a*) *May* can replace *can* in

[66]   You can drive my car;

but would then refer only to permission.

(*b*) Similarly, *may* can replace *can* in example [71]:

[71c]   May I borrow your pen, please?

May would there sound more hesitant than *can* and, to some people, more polite. A normal answer to *May I . . . ?* would be *Yes, of course you may* or *No you may not.*

(*c*) In *can v may* in (*a*) and (*b*), *can* might be considered as an unmarked form, frequently used in everyday conversation, while *may* is often a marked form deliberately used to stress the fact that *permission* is being sought and granted.

262   (*a*) In the secondary function, *may* is very often used. Whereas *can* in **254** refers to one possibility that is open, *may* suggests that there are two or more possibilities, both or all of which are worth considering. Thus:

[83]   This may be the answer

(*may* there would be stressed) suggests that the answer referred to is possibly the right one but that there are other possible answers. In [83], *may* refers to the present. It refers to future in

[84]   I may be late home this evening,

which means 'Perhaps I will be, perhaps not'.

(*b*) In this sense, *may not* is also often used. But the interrogative is best avoided. *Might this be the answer?* would be a normal interrogative transformation for [83]; while *May I be late this evening?* asks for permission to come home late, as in **261**. An acceptable question related to [84] would be

[84a]   Will you (*or* Are you likely to) be late this evening?

May Have-ed

263   Here again, the speaker makes a present assumption about the pre-present or the past. Thus:

[85]   He's late (*or* He was late). He may have been delayed by fog.

means 'I think one of the possible explanations of his lateness is that he has been delayed by fog.'

Might

264   *Might* is only the Past tense of *may* in indirect speech, as in

[66a]   You said I might drive your car

or

[84a]   He said he might be home late.

In direct speech, *You might drive my car* is not a translation of *You may drive* . . . into the past: the past equivalent of *You may drive it* would be *You could have driven it* (see example [78] in **259**).

265   *Might* expresses the maximum degree of hesitancy in requests for permission, e.g.

[71*c*]   Might I borrow your pen, please?

A polite answer to that request would be *Certainly*. Vague possibility, rather than positive permission, would be suggested by *Yes, you might*, while *No you might not* would be an abrupt refusal.

266   In the secondary function, *might* expresses the minimum degree of certainty in an assumption, as in *That might be the answer but I doubt it*. For *Might this be the answer?* see **262** (*b*). In *You know what the answer is: you might tell me* (stressed *tell*), the speaker is suggesting that the person addressed *should* give the answer.

Might Have-ed

267   (*a*) Here the speaker is, very hesitantly, making a present assumption about the pre-present or the past:

[85a]   A. I can't imagine why he is (*or* was) late.
        B. Nor can I. He might have been delayed by fog, or he
            might have had an accident.

(*b*) In [85a], perhaps there was an accident, perhaps not. In

[85b]   He might have been killed,

perhaps he was, or has been killed, perhaps not. But in

[86]   You were lucky. You might have been killed,

obviously the person addressed is not dead, but the chances of his being killed were considerable. In

[87]   You knew the answer. You might have told me (see **266**),

the speaker is expressing regret at not having been told sooner.

[88]   It was terribly cold in that house. I might have been in the Arctic,

does not mean that the speaker had been in the Arctic but that the temperature in the house seemed as low as it would have been in the Arctic Circle. Finally, when we say

[89]   Life is full of might-have-beens,

we mean that many things in life could or should have happened but have not actually taken place.

Might (or May) as Well; Had Better, Would Rather/Sooner

268   These modal-type expressions frequently occur in everyday conversation. *Might* (or *May*) *as well* suggests, or agrees to, a course of action, as in

[90]   A. Here comes a bus. We might as well take it.
         B. Yes, we might as well.

It can also suggest that a different course of action would be preferable:

[91]   A. How slow this bus is! We might as well walk.
         B. Yes, we might as well have gone on walking.

This construction does not occur in the interrogative or negative, but the verb following it can be negated:

[92]   A. It's impossible to bring our car into town these days.
         B. No, we might (just) as well not have one.

However, *it might be as well to* can have an interrogative form, e.g. *Might(n't) it* (or more formally *Might it not*) *be as well to consult a lawyer?*

269   *Had better* suggests a course of action that seems advisable, *would rather* (or *would sooner*) a course that the speaker prefers:

[93]   A. You've done enough. I think you'd better stop.
         B. No, I'd rather go on a little longer.

The verb following *had better* and *would rather* can be negated, e.g. *You'd better not stop. I'd rather not go on.* Other possible transformations are: *Hadn't we better ask? Would* (or *Wouldn't*) *you rather let me drive?* But the full range of normal negative, interrogative and negative-interrogative transformations (see **210**) does not apply to the constructions in these two paragraphs.

Need and Dare

270 *Need* is used as a modal verb to express an attitude toward unfulfilled activity (but see **212** (*g*)), or as a 'full verb', as in

[94] Do you need this piece of paper? Someone needs/needed it.

There may be a distinction between *We need not stay*, i.e. we are not obliged to (see **248**) and *We don't need to stay*, meaning 'It isn't necessary for us to stay.' Note also that *You needn't have done that* suggests that you have done something unnecessarily, while *You didn't need to do it* means that, whether you have done it or not, there was no obligation or necessity for the action. Thus, if I am invited to a party and take my hostess a large bunch of flowers, she might say either

[95] Oh, you didn't need to do that,

in which case SPPC is at the point in past time when I bought the flowers, or

[96] Oh, you needn't have done that

in which case SPPC is at point now (cp. **158**).

271 *Dare* is likewise both a modal and an ordinary, non-modal verb followed by the infinitive, with or without *to* (see **212** (*g*)). In its modal form, *daren't* can be used for used present and past, thus:

Present I daren't look down *or* I don't dare (to). . . .
Past I daren't look down *or* I didn't dare (to). . . .

The negative is carried over from the main clause to the subordinate in *I'm not sure that I dare go in*. The modal *dare* occurs exceptionally in the affirmative in *I dare say you're right*.

CHAPTER 7

Verb and Adjective Patterns

272 Although the basic information in this chapter belongs to the 'solid core' of English grammatical facts (see **11**), it is included as an essential preliminary to the chapters on the infinitive and the *-ing*, and on the section of phrasal verbs in Chapter 9.

273 Every English sentence and clause is constructed on one of five patterns:

Pattern	*Explanation*	*Example*
1. SV	Subject + Verb	The ghost disappeared
2. SVC	S + V + Complement	This is my husband
3. SVO	S + V + Object	He makes watches
4. SVOO	S + V + Indirect Object + Direct Object	He gave me this beautiful watch
5. SVOC	S + V + Object + Complement	He made me happy

274 It can easily be seen from **273** that the difference between one pattern and another lies in what, if anything, follows V: in other words it lies in the complementation (if any) of the verb. So what we are really concerned with is a difference in verb complementation or verb patterns.

275 **273** can be expanded and sub-divided as below. Explanations of the sub-divisions are given in **276**:

Pattern	*Sub-division*	*Example*
SV	1	The ghost disappeared
	a	I got up
	2	The door opened
	3	I watched, and listened
SVC	1	This is a story
	2	It is good
	3	It was there. It was yesterday.

SVO	1	Someone opened the door
	a	He put his hand in his pocket
	b	He took something out
	c	He had a gun
	2	I listened to his voice
	3	I wanted to scream
	4	I wanted him to go away
	5	I longed for someone to come
	6	I stopped trembling
	7	I remember you(r) coming
	8	I heard the bell ring
	9	We heard a dog barking
	10	We found the way blocked by a truck
	11	I said (that) we should go to the police
	12	I suggested that Dick (should) go
	13	I asked if (*or* whether) he had gone
	14	I wondered where you were
SVOO	1	My father gave me this watch
	2a	He gave this watch to me
	b	My mother made this scarf for me
	3	Tell me about your home
	4	Take care of your books
	5	He persuaded us that we were wrong
	6	Please inform me if you are coming
	7	Tell me when you will arrive
SVOC	1	We have appointed you Chairman
	2	The islanders paint their houses white
	3	You consider him guilty
	4	I regard him as innocent
	5	Did you mistake me for someone else?
	6	I consider it a shame/wrong to say that. I consider it a shame/wrong that he should be blamed

276 Explanations of sub-divisions:

SV 1: A good dictionary will indicate whether a verb can be used intransitively. Other verbs in SV 1 include *ache, come, fall, rise.*

1a: *Get* cannot be used intransitively without an adverbial particle (e.g. *up*) or adverbial adjunct (e.g. *into the car*). Other verbs requiring an adverbial include *lie* (e.g. *on the ground*) and *live* somewhere, at some time, somehow.

2: Obviously, someone or something caused the door to open. See SVO 1. Verbs that can be used similarly include *close, hurt, move, ring, stop, turn*.

3: I watched something (or someone), and *watch* can also be used in SVO 1. The same applies to *ask, answer, drink, eat, forget, read, write* and other verbs. But *listen, look* and *wait* will require a preposition before they can be used transitively: see SVO 2.

SVC 1: The verb in SVC is a copula, or linking verb. It can refer to an unchanging state of affairs (e.g. *be, resemble, sound*), in which case it will not occur in the progressive (**133** (*c*)); or to a change of state (*become*), in which case there is no restriction on the use of the progressive. C in SVC 1 is a noun.

2: Here, C is an adjective. Verbs referring to a change of state include the so-called inchoative verbs, as in *fall* (*sick*), *get* (*tired*), *go* (*mad*), *grow* (*old*), *turn* (*pale*). Note that *get* is commonly used in SVC 2 but cannot occur in SVC 1.

3: Here, the complementation is an adverbial, usually of place, though it could be of time (e.g. *The concert is at 8 o'clock*).

SVO 1: Again, a good dictionary will indicate which verbs can be used transitively. They include *ask, answer, drink, eat* (see also SV 3), and *do, enjoy, make, manufacture* which are not used intransitively. All verbs in SVO 1, and SVO 1a and b can be put into the passive.

a: An adverbial (or sometimes an adjective, e.g. *Put your desk straight*) is obligatory after *place* and *put*; also after *lay* as in *lay something on the ground*.

b: Here, the adverb particle (*out*) can also come before the object, but not if the object is a personal pronoun (*me, you, him, her, it, us, them*).

c: *Have* in the sense of 'possess', and *lack* (i.e. not have) will not be found in the passive.

2: *Listen, look* and *wait* can occur in SV 3. In SVO, a preposition is required, e.g. *listen to* (*look at*/*wait for*) someone. *Look after* (i.e. take care of) only occurs in SVO. The same applies to *long for, part with* and *taste of*. V in SVO 2 is called a prepositional verb.

3: Other verbs complemented by *to* + infinitive are *agree, attempt, decide, fail, hope, need* (as a 'full verb') and *wish*. Note that *to* is optional after *dare*; and that (*can't*) *bear, begin, cease, continue, prefer, propose* can fit into SVO 3 or SVO 6, without any substantial change in meaning. *Deserve, forget, remember, try* can also be used in both SVO 3 and SVO 6, but with *different* meanings. Note that pattern SVO 3 can only be used when the subject and the time reference of the two verbs are the same (*I wanted. I was about to scream*: both past), or *I hope to go* (*I hope, I go*: both present). The pattern cannot be used, for example, to replace *I want you to go* or *I hope you will go* or *I hope I went to the right house*.

4: The object here is *him to go away*. I did *not* want *him*. The subject of *to go* is considered to be *he*. *Want* could be replaced by *expect, get, intend, mean, recommend, wish*. *Promise* fits into SVO 3 and 4; but in *I promise you to go away* the subject of *to go away* is *I*.

5: This is similar to SVO 4, but V is a prepositional verb as in SVO 2. *Long for* could be replaced by *arrange for, ask for, wait for*.

6: Other verbs complemented by *-ing* are *avoid, dislike, enjoy, fancy, finish*, (*can't*) *help, practise, suggest*. See notes on SVO 3. Note that *This wants* (*or needs*) *cleaning* means *This needs to be cleaned*.

7: Many of the verbs used in SVO 6 can also occur in SVO 7. The possessive form (*your, his, their, my, our, John's* etc.) is traditionally considered 'correct', though *you, him, them* etc. would now be widely used. The possessive *its* might occur instead of *it*, but *that's* would be unacceptable, e.g. *I remember that happening to me once*.

8: Either the bare infinitive or the *-ing* could occur when V is *feel, hear, notice, see, watch*. See **282**. But the *to*-infinitive is used in the passive: *The bell was heard to ring*.

9: See note on SVO 8. Only the *-ing* would occur in examples like *I found him smoking, They kept us waiting, We stopped the fire* (*from*) *spreading*; and in such examples the possessive form (*his, our* etc.) would be unacceptable.

10: Here, SVO is complemented by a past participle phrase (or clause). *Have* frequently occurs in this pattern, as in *I had my hair cut*.

11: Here O is a *that*-clause, which can be considered as an indirect statement. *That* is optional in short sentences on this pattern. See **236** example [55]. Like *say* are *believe, don't doubt, feel, find, find out, note, notice, point out, wish*.

12: O is here a proposal for future action. See **236** example [54]. Like *suggest* are *agree, ask, decide, insist, propose*.

13: Here O is an indirect *Yes/No* question; and *ask* could be replaced by *doubt, find out, forget, (don't) know, inquire, wonder*.

14: O is an indirect *Wh*-question, and *ask* is replaceable by *inquire, find out*, etc.

SVOO 1 & 2: Verbs fitting into SVOO 1 and 2a include *bring, fetch, grant, hand, lend, offer, owe, pass, pay, promise, read, sell, send, show, teach, tell, throw, write*. Those fitting into 1 and 2b include *book, build, buy, call, catch, change, choose, find, sleep, order, reserve, save, spare*.

2a: Note that *describe, explain, mention, say, suggest* fit into SVOO 2a but not into 1.

b: *We provided blankets for the refugees* could be reworded *We provided the refugees with blankets*.

3: Also in this pattern: *You asked me about my home. I informed him of the results. We congratulate you on your success*. Here, the prepositional phrase is closely linked with the verb, *ask, inform, congratulate*.

4: Here, the prepositional phrase is closely linked with the object, *care*. Similarly, *take advantage of something, pay attention to somebody*.

5: *Persuade* replaceable by *assure, convince, inform, remind, satisfy, tell*.

6 & 7: Also *remind* and *tell*.

SVOC 1: C is now the complement of O: You have become Chairman. In this pattern, we find *christen, crown, name, nominate*. With those verbs and *appoint*, two passives are possible: *You have been appointed (Chairman). A Chairman has been appointed*. We could replace *appointed* in the active voice by *made, declared, proclaimed, voted*; but then only one passive would be possible, i.e. *You have been made Chairman.*

2: The houses became white as a result. Note also *This will drive me mad. Keep your feet warm. Wipe the windows clean.*

3: We could insert *to be* after *consider*; and could re-word the example *You consider that he is guilty.* C could also be a noun, e.g. *a criminal.*

4: *Regard* replaceable by *count, describe, look on.*

5: *Mistake* replaceable by *take.*

6: In the pattern SVOC, O could be *-ing*, as in *I consider cheating dishonest*, but it could not be an infinitive or a *that*-clause. Instead, O is expressed by *it*, and the infinitive or *that*-clause comes after C, as in the example for SVOC 6.

Adjective Patterns

277 In SVC, when C is an adjective it frequently has, and some-times must have, its own complementation. Complementation is structurally optional in *I am afraid (of snakes)* but obligatory in *I was aware of the danger.*

278 Adjective patterns can take three basic forms:

1. Adjective + prepositional phrase, as in **277**;
2. Adjective + *to*-infinitive, as in *afraid to jump*;
3. Adjective + *that*-clause, as in *afraid (that) I might break my leg.*

We shall discuss the infinitive in the next chapter, and prepositions in Chapter 9. Meanwhile, note that in the pattern SVC, S is often an *It* that anticipates an infinitive or *that*-clause, as in *It is a pity to spoil your picture. It's very sad that you are leaving us.*

This construction may require a putative *should*, as in *It is right that we should tell him the truth* (**236**).

CHAPTER 8

Infinitive or -ing

279 The problems here are to know

(*a*) whether to use the infinitive without *to* (*I must go*) or the *to*-infinitive (*I want to go*);

(*b*) whether to use the infinitive (*I refuse to go*; *I prefer to go*) or the verb ending in *-ing* (*I enjoy going, I prefer going*).

The Infinitive or -ing after Verbs

280 These are mainly questions of plain fact. We must become familiar—through hearing and reading the language or through exercises—with a variety of patterns and constructions such as were set out in Chapter 7. We can only accept the facts that:

(*a*) the bare infinitive is used after *do, does, did*; after *will, would, shall, should, can, could, may, might, might as well, had better, would rather, would sooner*; after *let*, as in *let go*, and *make*, as in *make do*; and in verb pattern SVO 8, *I heard the bell ring*;

(*b*) the *to*-infinitive occurs after *ought, used* (**172**), *have* (**246**) and *be* (**247**); and in verb patterns SVO 3, 4, 5 and SVOC 6, as in Chapter 7;

(*c*) the *-ing* occurs in SVO 6, 7 and 9;

(*d*) there is no option to replace the infinitive by *-ing* in *I hope to go*, or to replace the *-ing* by the infinitive in *I enjoy going*. The same is true of other such constructions which a good dictionary or reference grammar should indicate;

(*e*) we can say *We began to sing* or *We began singing* with no substantial change of meaning;

(*f*) we can say *I heard her sing* or *I heard her singing*, with a change of emphasis; and

(*g*) we can say *I remembered to go* which does not mean the same as *I remembered going*; and

(*h*) only the *-ing* form, not the infinitive, follows a preposition or a prepositional verb (SVO 2). Thus *Let's talk about fishing. He earns his living by translating. Take these pills before and after eating.*

138

Kindly refrain from smoking. Succeed in climbing. Suspected of cheating. Fond of reading. Tired of standing etc. etc. Note *look forward to going* and *object to smoking*, where *to* is a preposition, and *want to go*, where *to* is an infinitive marker, not a preposition. Note also the difference between *I'm used* (i.e. *accustomed*) *to waiting* and *I used to wait* (as in **172**).

281   We can trace three differences in meaning between the infinitive and the -*ing*. They may help to explain why the infinitive has become adopted in one pattern, while the -*ing* is adopted in another; and they can help us to decide which form to use when there is a choice.

282   First, the infinitive may refer either to the activity in general or to the act completed, in contrast with an -*ing* which refers to activity in progress. This distinction is similar to that between **O** and **U** in **137**, thus:

I saw him jump   I saw him running away
Fig. 33   Fig. 34

Examples:

   [1]   I saw the man jump.   (**I O**)
   [2]   I saw him running away.   (**I U**)
   [3]   I heard the dog bark.   (**I O**)
   [4]   I have often heard it bark.   (**S O**)
   [5]   I heard it barking all night.   (**S U**)

In those examples, *jump* is more precise than *jumping* if the speaker is referring to one completed act; *running* is better than *run* if the speaker is referring to the continuous action; *bark* refers to one sound, *barking* to a series of barks. Similarly, *I prefer to walk* could refer to the activity in general, while *I prefer walking* emphasises the continuous action. It is difficult to see such a distinction between *begin to run* and *begin running*: what is fairly certain is that *beginning running*, with its repetition of -*ings*, would be avoided. The chances are that after *begin, start, cease* and *continue* most users of English would choose the infinitive or the -*ing* by accident, or for the sake of euphony, rhythm or variety.

283   Activity having duration is, or can be, clearly emphasised by the *-ing* in *enjoy swimming. Do you mind waiting? Keep (on) walking. Go on reading. I dislike people pushing behind me in a queue.*

284   Second, the *-ing* may refer to activity in progress, as in **282**, while the infinitive refers to a new act in a chain of events, as in

Fig. 35

Examples:

    [6] I like dancing (*i.e. the activity*).
    [7] Would you like to dance?

Like, love, hate, prefer can be followed by either the infinitive or the *-ing*, as in *I love to lie* (or *I love lying*) *in the sun*: perhaps to some speakers and writers *lying* rather than *to lie* would emphasise the duration of the sun-bathing, the continuous feeling of having the sun warming one's skin. But normally *would like, would love, would hate, would prefer* point to a new act in a chain of events and are followed by the infinitive. However, *would prefer* could be followed by *-ing* if it referred to activity in progress, having duration, as in *Which would you prefer, lying on the beach in the sun, or lying for days in a tiny space-ship?*

285   A distinction between new act (infinitive) and activity having duration (*-ing*) might be noticeable in the following pairs:

    [8] (*a*) It is a great pleasure to be with you tonight.
        (*b*) It is a great pleasure being with you tonight.
    [9] (*a*) The climbers made another attempt to reach the top.
        (*b*) The climbers made another attempt at reaching the top.

There is a greater difference between (*a*) and (*b*) in

    [10] (*a*) We were interested to hear your news.
         (*b*) We are not interested in hearing gossip.

In [10] (*a*), we are interested in a new development. In [10] (*b*), we are not interested in the activity of listening to gossip. The difference is perhaps greater still in

    [11] (*a*) Now let us try to turn the key to the right.
         (*b*) Now let us try turning the key to the right.

In [11] (*a*), *try to turn* would often be replaced in spoken English by *try and turn*, which refers to two separate acts: one, try; two, turn. In [11] (*b*), *turning* refers to a process; and the example means 'Let us experiment by turning the key to the right', in order to see if we can unlock the door *that* way. The difference is even greater in

[12]   (*a*) They deserve to shoot first.
     (*b*) They deserve shooting first.

[12] (*a*) means *They have earned the right to be the first to shoot* while [12] (*b*) means *They ought to be shot* (*before something else happens*).

286   Third, the infinitive again points to a move forward in a series of events, while the *-ing* looks backwards to previous activity in progress or even to a previous act completed. Here, the two members of a pair may have quite different meanings:

[13]   (*a*) I remembered to telephone the doctor.
     (*b*) I remembered telephoning the doctor.

[13] (*a*) means: First I remembered what I had to do, then I telephoned. [13] (*b*) means: I telephoned the doctor, and remembered doing so. We could also say [13] (*c*) *I remembered having telephoned the doctor*. To be precise, I would use [13] (*b*) if I meant that I recalled the act of telephoning, and [13] (*c*) if I meant that I recalled that the act had been performed. There is a similar difference in

[14]   (*a*) I usually forget to sign my letters.
     (*b*) I shall never forget seeing Fujiyama by moonlight.

[14] (*a*) suggests that I forget that I have to sign my letters and therefore do not sign them, while [14] (*b*) suggests that I shall not forget an event that occurred in the past. *I forgot having signed that letter* would emphasise the perfective which would be made clear in *I forgot that I had signed it*. Another such pair is

[15]   (*a*) I regret to tell you that I shall be away.
     (*b*) I regret telling you that I shall be away.

In [15] (*a*) I regret and now I tell you. In [15] (*b*) I (have) told you, and now I regret it. Once more, *I regret having told you* would emphasise the perfective interpretation of (*b*).

287   The *-ing* clearly refers to a process on which the speaker is looking back in *I stopped writing, finished working, gave up smoking*.

On the other hand, the infinitive refers to a new act in *I stopped to write my name in the visitors' book*.

288   In *I stopped to write*, the infinitive is not a complementation of the verb. *I stopped* + infinitive can be analysed as SV plus an adverbial adjunct of purpose. Such an adjunct can be added to any of the verb patterns given in Chapter 7, so long as the verb refers to an action that can be performed voluntarily and purposefully. Thus:

[16]   I stopped the car to look at the radiator.
[17]   We sent her some flowers to thank her for the party.

The adverbial adjunct of purpose could be made clearer by inserting *so as*, or more formally *in order*, before the *to*-infinitive.

289   Compare example [16] above with

[18]   I stopped the car to find that the radiator was almost empty,

where *to find* could be replaced by *and found*—a new act in the chain of events, expressing consequence rather than purpose.

Infinitive after Adjectives

290   As we saw in **277**, an adjective acting as C in SVC (i.e. an adjective used predicatively) can be complemented by an infinitive. The meaning of this complementation is by no means always the same. We can distinguish at least seven different types, as the examples below and the re-wording of them will indicate:

1. *He is eager to go*, i.e. He very much wants to go. There the adjective expresses an attitude, on the part of the person mentioned, towards something that has not happened, i.e. towards a possible future event; and the infinitive could not be replaced by *-ing*. Instead of *eager* we could say *able, anxious, determined, keen*, etc.
2. *He is certain to go*, i.e. It is certain that he will go. Again, *to go* is a possible future event. But here *certain* is expressing the speaker's own attitude towards the future. (Note the difference between *Tom is certain to win* (the speaker is certain that he will) and *Tom is certain of winning* (Tom himself is certain that he will).)
3. *He is happy to go*, i.e. He is happy because he is going or because he knows he is. *He was happy to go*, because he went.

Happy could be replaced by *delighted, fortunate, glad, proud, sorry,* etc. The infinitive could be replaced by an -*ing* clause that refers to continuing action, as in *He is very happy playing with his children again.*

4. *He is sensible to go,* i.e. He is being sensible, or acting sensibly, by going; in other words, it is sensible of him to go. *Sensible* could only be replaced by adjectives which indicate a way of behaviour, e.g. *clever, kind, polite, rude, selfish, silly, wise.* Note that *He was kind to write to me like that* could be reworded *He was kind writing to me like that*; or *He kindly wrote to me,* not *He wrote to me kindly.*

5. *He is quick to go on errands for me,* i.e. He quickly agrees to go on errands, or *He is quick going on errands.* Instead of *quick* we could say *hesitant, prompt, slow, willing.*

6. *He is difficult to amuse,* i.e. It is difficult for anyone to amuse him. The -*ing* could not replace the infinitive in that pattern, which could also be used for *easy, hard, hopeless, interesting.* We could use the pattern for an inanimate subject, as in *This car is easy to drive,* i.e. one can easily drive it.

7. If we replace *This car* in that last example by *It,* we get *It is easy to drive.* There, *it = this car.* But *It is easy to drive* could also mean *To drive* (or *Driving*) *is easy,* and in that case *It* stands for *to drive.*

Infinitive after Nouns

291 Generally speaking, the pattern *agree (arrange, decide, determine, fail, hesitate, offer, plan, promise, threaten, wish,* etc.) + *to*-infinitive (SVO 3) can be matched by *agreement (arrangement, decision, determination, failure, hesitation, offer, plan, promise, threat, wish,* etc.) + *to*-infinitive as in

[19] We agreed to share the profits; and our agreement to share the profits still stands.

Similarly *anxious (inclined, ready, reluctant, willing) to please* could be matched by *anxiety (inclination, readiness, reluctance, willingness) to please.* There are few exceptions, e.g.

[20] We had hoped to finish this work by the end of this month, but there is no hope of doing so now.

[21] Some people like to read, others prefer to watch television, others have a preference for sitting and talking.

292 An infinitive can replace a relative clause after a noun, as in

[22]   Here is an interesting book to read (*i.e. an interesting book that you or anyone else can read*).

[23]   Here is another book for you to look at.

In [23] *for you to look at* means 'that you can look at', *for* being used to specify the subject of the infinitive clause. Other examples are:

[24]   He is a man to trust (*or to be trusted*)

i.e. He is a man whom one can trust; and

[25]   He was the first man to fly across the Atlantic,

i.e. the first man who flew across it.

An infinitive can similarly modify an indefinite pronoun:

[26]   Would you like something to eat?

Not To, To Be-ing, To Have-ed

293   The negative, progressive and perfective of the infinitive are illustrated in the following dialogue:

[27]   A. I'm sorry not to be able to stay longer. I'm sorry to be going so soon.
        B. Yes, and I'm sorry you have to go. I'm sorry to have seen so little of you.

In *I am sorry to go* the subject of *am* is also the subject of *go*, and the time reference is the same in both parts of the sentence (cp. note on SVO 3 in **276**). However, instead of *I'm sorry (that) I have seen* (or *I saw*) *so little of you*, we can use the perfect infinitive, *to have seen*. The perfect infinitive often gives trouble after *would like* and *would have liked*. Note these examples:

[28]   (*a*) I would like (now) to see that exhibition (now).
        (*b*) I would like (now) to have seen it (before now).
        (*c*) I would have liked (then) to see it (then).
        (*d*) I would have liked (then) to have seen it (before then).

Infinitive or -ing as Subject, Object or Complement

294   We have already seen, in Chapter 7 and in **279**, that both the infinitive and the *-ing* can act as object of a verb; but certain verbs take only the infinitive as the object, while others take only the *-ing*. Both forms can act as subject of a sentence, as in

[29]   To learn (*or* learning) a new language is difficult.

However, the -*ing* is more likely to begin a sentence than the infinitive; and *It*, as subject, frequently anticipates the infinitive, e.g.

[30]   It is difficult to learn a new language.

Both forms could act as a complement of *be*, as in

[31]   My greatest pleasure is lying (*or* to lie) in the sun.

-ing Clauses

295   *Lying in the sun*, as in [31] can be described as an -*ing* clause in which the continuous process of sun-bathing is emphasised. It is similarly emphasised in

[32]   Lying in the sun like this, I feel perfectly at ease.

There *I* is assumed to be the subject of *lying*. I am lying here, and I feel perfectly at ease. Note that

[33]   *Lying here on the sand, the sun feels very warm

is unacceptable, because it is not the sun that is lying. But there would be no objection to

[34]   Running to the water, I feel the sand burning beneath my feet,

where it is clear that I am running and the sand is burning.

296   While the link between the -*ing* form of the verb and the progressive is strong, and often obvious, there are occasions when an -*ing* clause bears no relation to the progressive aspect at all. We have already seen (in 143) that it is difficult to imagine a single act of jumping in an uncompleted state. Yet there is only one quick jump in

[35]   Jumping into his car, he drove off in pursuit.

There, we are concerned with two consecutive acts—he jumped, then he drove; and the first is reported in a subordinate position in the sentence. This throws the spot-light onto the action reported by the finite verb (*drove*). Note that in [35], as the jumping came first, the -*ing* clause must precede the main clause. But in

[36]   Ignoring the traffic lights, he raced in pursuit,

the -*ing* refers to a process in which the driver is engaged as he goes along, as well as expressing an action that is formally subordinated to *he raced*. The actions here are not consecutive, as they are in [35]:

they are simultaneous, and *ignoring the traffic lights* could either precede or follow the main clause.

297   The *-ing* can even be used with verbs which would rarely, if ever, be used in the progressive, thus:

[37]   Knowing Dick so well, I can thoroughly recommend him.

However, a difference in the use of the *-ing* in [36] and [37] becomes apparent when we expand the examples as follows:

[36a]   Ignoring the traffic lights as he was (ignoring the traffic lights).

[37a]   Knowing Dick as I do (know him).

298   A confusion often occurs between *amusing* and *amused*, *interesting* and *interested*, and similar pairs that can be used adjectivally. The problem can easily be resolved in the following way:

[38]   (*a*) This story amuses/bores/fascinates/interests/me.
     (*b*) It is amusing/boring/fascinating/interesting.
     (*c*) I am amused by/bored by/fascinated by/interested in it.

299   Whether the *-ing* form of the verb is what is traditionally called a present participle or a gerund is often an academic question, of no great importance. However, there are occasions when it is helpful to distinguish between two kinds of *-ing*, calling one a participle, the other a gerund, for convenience.

(*a*)   [39]   Standing in the sun I feel too hot.
     [40]   Standing in the sun makes me giddy.

Standing in [39], 'agreeing' with *I*, could be called a participle. *Standing* in [40], equivalent to a noun, could be called a gerund.

(*b*) *Running* in *a running stream* (i.e. a stream that runs or is running) could be called a participle; and *running* and *stream* are equally stressed. In *running shoes* (i.e. shoes used for running) it could be called a gerund; and *running* bears a strong stress while *shoes* does not.

(*c*) If in a noun phrase there is a series of modifiers coming before the head-word, then a participle used as an adjective would come before a gerund, as in *This charming French writing desk*.

Having-ed, Having Been-ed

300   These constructions sometimes seem difficult to use, though they need not be as the following pairs illustrate:

[41] (*a*) I have travelled round the world and have made many friends.

    (*b*) Having travelled round the world, I have made etc.

[42] (*a*) You have been invited to the reception formally and you ought to send a formal reply.

    (*b*) Having been invited to the reception formally, you ought etc.

[41] (*a*) and [41] (*b*) have the same meaning; so have [42] (*a*) and [42] (*b*).

CHAPTER 9

Prepositions, Adverb Particles and Phrasal Verbs

Prepositions

301 The prepositions express relationships in space between one thing and another, and relationships in time between events. They might be considered basically as applications of the ideas contained in the scheme:

Fig. 36

to something having no, or an unspecified, dimension; to something having one dimension; having two dimensions; or three dimensions. In space, let us call something with no, or unspecified dimension, a point; with one dimension, a line, two dimensions, a surface, three, a space or area. (Be careful to distinguish between 'space (not time)' and 'a space, something having volume'.) In time, we can imagine a point of time, or a period. In using the prepositions we are concerned not so much with objective measurements, i.e. with the actual dimensions of the things to which we are referring, as with how we imagine them to be at the time of speaking. Thus we can imagine a town as a point on the map, as a surface to go across, or as a space we live in or walk through. Moreover, a point itself, seen through a microscope, may appear to have surface which can be covered or space which can be penetrated.

302 It is possible to fit a great number of usages into this scheme, and there is much to be said, in teaching the prepositions, for beginning with those usages which fall into a scheme of this kind easily. On the other hand, many usages are very difficult to systematise. That is not surprising. Some of the relationships we want to express are very complex. We express them by little words whose full meaning could only be explained in long circumlocutions. Moreover, the number of these little words is limited, and each may have to serve a variety of purposes. Nevertheless, the use of prepositions in English can be remarkably, almost geometrically, precise, and the student would be well advised to be as clear about them as he can, without forcing natural usage into an artificial framework.

No, or Unspecified, Dimension: To, At, From

303 Movement in the direction of a point is expressed by *to*; in the opposite direction, by *from*. Imagine two things, X and Y, occupying two different positions; and *imagine* the position of Y to be a point or to be of unspecified dimension. If X moves so as to occupy more or less the same position as Y, then we say that X moves *to* Y. So X is now *at* Y. If we now remove X, we take it *from* Y. Thus

Fig. 37

Remember that *to* and *from* express movement; *at*, no movement. All three can be applied to a point both in space and in time: *This train goes from London to Edinburgh in six hours, stopping only at York. Your lesson is from nine to* (or *till*) *ten in the morning: it starts promptly at nine.* (But *Your lesson will last till ten*—not *to*, when *from* is omitted.)

304 Other examples of *to, at* and *from*:

(*a*) *Go to bed. Listen to me. Does this book belong to you? Best wishes to you all. I passed* (*my examination*), *thanks to you. Be kind to animals, don't be cruel to them. Stick to your principles.* Note that the infinitive marker *to* frequently points *forward* (———→) to a fresh act in the course of events: see particularly **284–286**.

(*b*) *I live at this address, at number 30. At what time shall we meet? I'm busy at the moment.* Notice especially:

(i) the idea of stationary relationship with unspecified dimension in *I'm sitting at a desk, at a table, at the window; I'm standing at the door.* Contrast: *Your book is on, or in, the desk, on the table.*

Who stuck that paper on the window?; *There's a name painted on the door*;

(ii) the same idea applied to a general concept (see **98** (*c*)): *at work*, *at play*, *at rest*, *at fault*, *at peace*, *at war* (cp. *in the war*, to emphasise the period, and also to specify which war), *at sea* (cp. *on the sea*, i.e. on the surface, and *in the sea*, i.e. in the volume of water), *at night* (cp. *in the night*, to emphasise the period, and either to specify which night, or to distinguish night from day);

(iii) concentration on the final point of the movement: *aim at*, *arrive at*, *laugh at*, *shoot at*, *throw at*. (Note: *throw the ball to me*, i.e. in my direction, *not at me*, so as to hit me.) Similarly, *point to the blackboard*, but *don't point at other people—it's rude*.

(*c*) *How far is the bus stop from here? Let's escape from it all. Tell me the worst, don't hide it from me. No one can prevent me* (*from*) *finding out. To be absent from work. Refrain from spitting.*

Towards, As Far As

305   *To* envisages completed movement and suggests that X actually reaches Y, or will reach Y unless prevented. Movement in the direction of Y, without the idea of completion, is expressed by *towards*. This applies only to space, though we sometimes say *towards* (*six o'clock*) to mean *about or nearly then*. To emphasise the length of the journey to Y, which is eventually reached, we say *X goes as far as Y*.

Till (or Until), Since

306   *As far as* is used only for space. To emphasise length of time, eventually concluded, we say *till* or *until* the final point. *If you want a walk, I'll come with you as far as the shops, but I am not ready yet—I shall be busy till five o'clock. Since*, as we saw in **158**, means 'in the progress of time from a specified point in the past until the speaker's point of primary concern', whether SPPC is present or past, *I have not seen him since Thursday. Yesterday was the hottest day since 1925.*

(Away) From, Far, Near

307   *From* (with space) is reinforced by *away*, which stresses the idea of the separation of the two positions held by X and Y. Thus *X is at Y. Now it moves away from Y*. When X occupies a different position from Y, and is stationary, then we say

$$X \text{ is} \begin{cases} \text{so many inches (miles, etc.)} \\ \text{some distance, a long way} \\ \text{not far}^1 \end{cases} (\text{away}) \text{ from } Y$$

If Y is mentioned, *from* must precede it, and *away* is optional. To emphasise the *shortness* of the distance between X and Y, we say *X is near Y.*

For

308   To express the object or purpose of the *to* movement, or to indicate the person or thing affected by it, we can use *for*. Thus:

(*a*) *The train for Paris* (the train that is planned to go to Paris), *a ship bound for Rio, We're just starting* (*off* or *out*) *for the north, going for a holiday. Go for a walk, a swim, a drive, for pleasure, for what purpose? What for? We shall be out for dinner, we're having chicken for dinner.*

(*b*) *This is a present for you*—I bought it to give to you. And this *is for John. I'm doing this for you* (for your benefit, or on your behalf). *I'm asking* (*calling, looking, longing, sending*) *for you*—the object and purpose of those actions. *I'm sorry for you* (I'm giving you my sympathy). Notice the extension of this usage in *I'm for you* (giving you my support), *I'm for the motion* (giving my support to a proposal in a debate).

(*c*) With time, *for* + a measurement of time can indicate the proposed, expected or completed length of the period during which an action takes place: *We shall be staying in Scotland for three weeks. You've been learning English for six years. You were at school for twelve years. We walked for two hours. I shall love you for ever.*

309   *For* can also indicate exchange; e.g. *I bought this for ten dollars. May I change it for a slightly smaller one? You couldn't get anything smaller for love nor money. Thank you for your help.*

Of

310   *From*, like *to*, basically expresses a physical movement, clearly traceable. The idea of *from* can be expressed in a more general, abstract way by *of*, to indicate origin or one of the relationships defined in **311** below. Examine the following pairs:

---

[1] Note that in short sentences *far* will often occur in the interrogative (*Is it far?*) and negative (*It isn't far*), but is avoided in a short affirmative sentence (*It's a long way*), unless *far* is modified by an adverb (*It's quite far*).

[1] (*a*) This cupboard was made from (*or* out of) an old wooden packing-case (*a specific, clearly traceable transition*).   (*b*) It is therefore made of wood. (*The transition from substance to object is less obvious, more general.*)

[2] (*a*) These are all vegetables from (*or* out of) my garden.   (*b*) They are the fruits of the earth, results of my labours.

[3] (*a*) Fill the bucket from the well.   (*b*) The bucket's full of water.

[4] (*a*) Take some paper from my writing-pad.   (*b*) Have you taken a piece of my writing-pad?

[5] (*a*) Have a chocolate—take one from the bottom layer.   (*b*) I won't have another of yours—you have one of mine.

[6] (*a*) Your holiday didn't do you much good—you've lost all the colour from your cheeks.   (*b*) Colour of eyes. Colour of hair (*quoted from my passport*).

[7] (*a*) I could make you a vase from this lump of clay.   (*b*) Are you making a fool of me, making fun of me?

311 An important function of *of* is to express the relationship between the part and the whole, e.g. *some of all, a quarter of an hour.* Variations of this are: the relationships between the member and the body to which that member belongs (*the leg of a chair, the top of the stairs, the secretary of the club*); between a quality and something possessing it (*the beauty of the landscape*); between a condition and something in that condition (*the health of a nation*); between an aspect and the thing we are considering (*a view of the summit*: cp. *a view from the summit*); and so on. *Of* is like the line in a fraction in mathematics. In $\frac{3}{8}$, $\frac{8}{3}$, $\frac{x}{y}$, $\frac{y}{x}$, the line tells us the relationship between 3 and 8, x and y, so long as we understand the significance of the order of the symbols, i.e. whether they come above or below the line. In *a brick of the house* (*Shakespeare lived in*) and *a house of brick*, the *of* indicates a similar relationship between *brick* and *house*, a relationship dependent on which word comes before *of* and which after it.

By, Beyond, Past, Before, After

312 Look again at Fig. 37. Suppose we alter the position of the arrows and the small circle, so that the diagram looks like this:

Fig. 38

The movement now is in one direction only, although it may stop at o. Suppose X moves, in space, from A to B. In the process, *X goes by the point Y*. At o, X is stationary: *it is then by the point Y*. Notice that it goes not only as far as Y (**305**) but also *beyond* it. To emphasise the fact that, in going by Y, X also goes beyond it, we can say that *X goes past Y*.

313 In time, the first arrow in **312** begins at A, which is *before Y*, and *ends by Y*. In this sense, *by* can be analysed to mean *in the progress of time ending about but not later than* the point of time mentioned. Compare *by* with *till* in the following pair of sentences:

[8] (*a*) I shall not be ready till five o'clock (*my not being ready will extend through a period ending at that point, when I shall be ready*).

    (*b*) I shall not be ready by five o'clock (*i.e. I shall not be ready in a period ending at five*).

Note that the verb in (*a*) must be one that refers to activity that can extend through a period of time, e.g. *I waited till five*. On the other hand, the verb in (*b*) can be a point-of-time verb, e.g. *We shall leave by five*.

314 In Fig. 38, B is *after* Y; in other words, at B, time has gone past Y, and in that sense *B is past Y*; thus *it is half past eleven, past my bedtime*. Continuous progress of time, past Y, then past a new point, Z, etc. can be said to go on *by day* and *by night*.

315 It may be stretching the imagination to fit *by* as an expression of *means* or *agency* into this scheme. If only for convenience and to complete the picture, I would classify this aspect of *by* as a relationship represented by the second part of the movement in **312**. It is easy enough to see that the train, in **303**, goes from London to Edinburgh *by* York. The next step is to see that the traveller goes from London to Edinburgh *by York*, and *by train*. In Fig. 38, Y is the means *by* which B is attained. (Compare this with *with*, **335**.) This could enable us to account for usages on the pattern of *by means of*, *by electricity*, and also *a book by Conan Doyle*, i.e. the medium by which the book was created. I would not pretend that it accounts for certain other usages, such as *This room measures 6 metres by 4.*

316   Examples of *by*:

(*a*) in space, continuous movement passing Y: *I always go by the post-office on my way to the station.*

(*b*) in space, fixed relationship with and very near Y: *He was sitting by the fire, by the open window, by his mother, by himself* (i.e. alone). For *walking along by the river*, see **320**.

(*c*) in space—means or agency: *We'll manage this somehow—by hook or by crook. To travel by car, by air, by sea. To send a message by ordinary mail, by telephone, by radio. To learn something by heart, by chance. Material made by hand, by machinery. 'Ode to a Nightingale', by John Keats.*

(*d*) in time, ending near, and not past, Y: *'Cobbler, cobbler mend my shoe, Get it done by half past two.' The concert will be over by ten.*

(*e*) in time, passing one stage after another: *To avoid being seen, they travelled by night, and lay hidden during the day.*

Round, About

317   X can go round Y,

(*a*) like a fence round a tree:

Fig. 39

(*b*) like a yacht sailing round a buoy:

Fig. 40

or (c) like a man walking round a corner:

Fig. 41

Around has the same meaning as *round,* and can be substituted for it for the sake of rhythm, e.g. to avoid two stressed syllables coming together. In space, *about,* as a concrete expression of **317** (a), is now out of fashion. Shakespeare's Julius Caesar said: '*Let me have men about me that are fat.*' In modern English, this would be '*I must have men around me*', or '*round about me*' if one wanted to reinforce the idea of having such men on every side. However, as an adverbial particle, *about* is still used in the sense of (a) and even of (b)—as in **343**. In the abstract, *about* commonly suggests *moving in any direction, or being in any position, in the vicinity of the point;* e.g. *think, talk, know, dream about the subject; tell me all about it; don't worry about it; what is it about? A book, or a lecture, about mountaineering* suggests a general treatment of the subject and freedom to wander a little from the point; whereas *a book, or a lecture, on new techniques in rock-climbing,* suggests concentration on a clearly defined field. In time, *I'll be there about six o'clock* is a common usage, expressing the idea of (a). We can also say *I'll be there around six o'clock.*

One Dimension: To, On, Off, From

318 Now apply the scheme to a line:

Fig. 42

Examples:

(a) *This road leads to the river, to the coast, to the frontier.*

(*b*) *London is on the River Thames. Brighton is on the coast. I'm on my way home. Am I on the right road for Y? Never stand on the edge of a cliff.* (Note, however: *Will there be a customs examination at the frontier?* i.e. at the point on the frontier where our road crosses it.)

(*c*) *You're not on the right road for X—but you're not far off it. The 'Titanic' was wrecked off the coast of Greenland. A man was killed last night when his car skidded off the road and crashed into a tree.*

(*d*) *Refugees fleeing from the frontier. Stand away from the edge.*

Along, Across

319   When we say *X is on the road to Y*, we are more concerned with X's position than with its movement. To emphasise the idea of movement following the course before it, we say *X is moving along the road to Y.* Thus:

Fig. 43

320   Apply the diagram in **312** to a line, either thus:

Fig. 44

or thus:

Fig. 45

Fig. 44 could represent *a man walking by* (or *beside*) *a river*, or *walking along by*, or *along beside, it*; or, at o, *a man standing by*, or *beside, the river.*

Fig. 45 could represent *a road running across the frontier*, or *a tree lying across the railway line.*

Behind, In Front Of

321   In the following situation

Fig. 46

A is behind B, and B is in front of A. This applies both when the arrow represents the line of vision of a speaker at X, and when it represents a line of advance along which A and B are moving in the direction indicated.

Two Dimensions: On (or Onto), On, Off

322 Movement in the direction of a surface, and reaching it, is expressed by *on*. To emphasise movement towards and then position on the surface, or the effort required to complete that process, we say *onto*. (This is sometimes written *on to*, which might be confused with the *on to* as in *We walked on to Rome* (**348**).) To indicate that X (moving or stationary) covers some or all of the surface Y, we use *on*. The opposite of *onto*, and the negative of *on* (i.e. *not on*) is *off*.

Fig. 47

The surface can be horizontal (e.g. the floor, the ceiling); it can be vertical (a wall); or lateral (a side). Examples:

(*a*) *Have you put the bread on the table?* (movement, but *onto* unnecessary). *This suitcase is terribly heavy. Can you help me lift it onto the bed?* (*onto* emphasising movement in that direction, then placing on the surface); *Hang the pictures on the wall.*

(*b*) *Is the bread on the table? How can I sleep with this suitcase on the bed? Don't run on the flower-beds. Keep on the right side of the law.*

(*c*) *Help me get this suitcase off the bed again. Keep your feet off the chairs.*

323 As we noticed with *talk about v talk on* (**317**), *on* concentrates on a more clearly defined field: a field is a surface having length and breadth. Moreover, while *X is at Y* suggests that X occupies more or less the same position as Y, without specifying dimension, *X is on Y* indicates that X covers some if not all of the actual surface of Y, or is supported by it, or attached to it. Example: *There was no policeman at the spot where the accident occurred, but the police were on the spot within two minutes,* i.e. they were standing on the actual scene of the accident. *To be at business* means to be at work in an office; *to go to New York on business* is to go there with a specified field of business to cover. One can be *at the point of leaving*; or *on the point of leaving*, like a runner on his marks. (The starter of a race calls out: '*On your marks—get set . . .*' and fires the starting-pistol.) *A fish, nibbling at your bait, is not yet on your hook.* From all this, it should be easy to understand *a hat on one's head, a house on the top of the hill, riding on horseback, standing on one's own feet*— and hence *to travel on foot.*

324 With time, note: *at six o'clock on a sunny day in June, on* covering a division of time intermediate between that associated with *at* and that with *in.* Similarly, *on Monday, on Tuesday,* etc., *on the morning (afternoon, evening) of the third day.* Observe the difference between *Where were you on the morning of November 19th?* i.e. on that precise date, and *On November 19th, I was working at my office in the morning, but went home feeling unwell in the afternoon* (see *in,* **329**).

325 *On* can therefore be used:

(*a*) with reference to a line, **318** (*b*);
(*b*) to show X moving towards, and reaching a surface, horizontal or vertical, **322** (*a*);
(*c*) to show X at rest, partially or wholly covering Y, or supported by it, **322** (*b*) and **323**; and
(*d*) with reference to time, in establishing the date of an event, precise to the day of the week or month.

326 *Upon* is sometimes substituted for *onto* (movement) and *on* (rest) in dignified or poetic language, for the sake of rhythm, or to suggest 'firmly on' or 'high up on'; cp, however, *up on,* **348**: *Upon* occurs in certain fixed expressions, like the exclamatory *upon my word*, *upon my soul*, though these may now be going out of fashion.

327 Other relationships with a surface are:

Fig. 48. A road running across the plain (cp. **320**, Fig. 45)

Fig. 49. The post-office is just across the road

Three Dimensions; In (or Into), In (or Inside), Out of, Outside

328 In space, movement in the direction of a space and penetrating it is expressed, simply, by *in*; but to mark the emphasis comparable to that expressed by *onto* we say *into* a space. To indicate that X occupies some or all of the space Y, we use *in*. The opposite of *into* is *out of*. The negative of the preposition *in* (i.e. *not in*) is *outside*. To emphasise the idea of *not outside* we use *inside*.

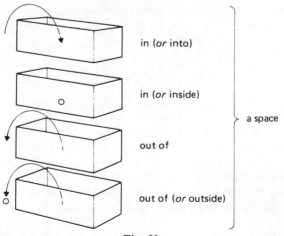

Fig. 50

Examples:

(*a*) *Put these books in your suitcase* (movement, but *into* unnecessary). *People started running into the building* (*into* emphasising the complete movement, and also necessary to avoid confusion with *running in the building* which might suggest running inside, not outside it).

(*b*) *Is my book in your suitcase? Shakespeare was born in England, in Warwickshire. I don't like swimming in muddy water, nor in the dark. Wait inside the car till the rain stops.*

(*c*) *They all rushed out of the building again when the explosion occurred.*

(*d*) *Outside the house, the crowd watched anxiously.*

In, Within

329 Whereas *X is on Y* suggests that Y *supports* X, *X is in Y* suggests that Y *encloses* X: in other words, Y has limits which hold X. Imagine and demonstrate the difference between *I place this coin on my hand* and *What have I got in my hand?* Such limits may enclose a surface-area; but in saying *in this area* (*district, region*), *in this city*, *in Africa*, etc., the emphasis is not on the supporting surface but on the space enclosed by certain limits. Emphasis on the idea of *in* certain limits and not outside them is contained in the word *within*, which can be used for space (*within an area*) or time (*within six days*).

330 There are many metaphorical applications of the above uses of *in*. Examples: *To be in debt, in love, in trouble, in good health. This book is written in English.*

In, During

331 *In* is used with a period of time, thus: *Classes start in October. He was born in 1846, in the nineteenth century. Rome was not built in a day*, i.e. it was not built within the limits of twenty-four hours. *I'll see you in ten minutes* (or *ten minutes' time*), means 'I'll see you at the end of ten minutes.' Note that the word *time* is only added to that last example when we mean 'so many minutes (hours, etc.) from now'. *He ran a mile in four minutes* means that his running took exactly that time. *During* is used to indicate the continuance or extent of a period, or of an event or series of events occurring within that period; e.g. *The entrance examinations will be held during*

September. During the examination, i.e. while it is in progress, *you cannot leave the room.* The difference between *in* and *during* might be shown thus:

An event takes place at   An event or series of events
this point in this period   takes place during this period
or during some other event

Fig. 51

332   Comparable with *passing by a point*, or *across a line or surface*, we have *through a space or period*, thus:

Knock a hole through the wall   All through the night

Fig. 52

Up, Down; Over, Under, Underneath; Above, Below, Beneath

333   *Up* (↑) and *down* (↓) should raise no difficulty; nor should <u>over</u> and <u>under</u>

Compare *a roof over one's head*, i.e. providing cover or protection, with *a hat on one's head*, i.e. touching, and supported by, its surface; similarly, compare *a fly on the ceiling*, i.e. attached to it and *a dog under the table*, i.e. covered by it. The idea of being physically covered up can be emphasised by *underneath* e.g. *I found this important letter underneath a pile of newspapers. Above* stresses the idea of *at a higher point* or *on a higher level*; *below, a lower point or level.* A swimmer has to keep his head *above water*: what is important is that his mouth should be at a higher level than the water's surface. A skin-diver must be careful not to go *below* a certain depth otherwise the pressure at that lower level will cause him serious injury. A man can be *above me* or *below me* in rank, without being *over me* or *under me*, i.e. without directly controlling me or having to obey my orders. Emphasis on the idea of the lowness of the level is contained in *beneath*, especially in poetic and metaphorical expressions, as in *beneath the waves, beneath contempt.*

334 *Over* and *under* express both rest and motion. *Over* often expresses the following movement:

Fig. 53

and often emphasises the idea of having arrived at the other side of an obstacle; e.g. '*The cow jumped over the moon*' and *You're over the line*, i.e. you've crossed it.

Relationships between Forces—With, Without, Against

335 Now consider relationships between the forces represented by the arrows in **301**, thus:

Fig. 54

Fig. 55

In Fig. 54, *X is going with Y*. The negative of this statement is, of course, *X is not going with Y*: in other words, *it is going without Y*. Physically, the opposite of it (Fig. 55), is *X is going against Y*. Note *Come and sit by* (or *with*) *me; and then come with me to the concert.* Note also the instrumental *with*, and compare it with the *by* of means or agency. When you *write with a pen*, your hand and pen proceed together.

336 On the other hand, when you *swim against the current*, you and the current are in conflict. Even when you are *leaning against the wall*, there is a force against you: if that force is not strong enough, the wall collapses. *One fights against temptation, struggles against fierce opposition, produces arguments against one's opponents* *in a debate.* Nevertheless—partly, perhaps, for reasons connected with the derivation of the word *with*—one can still *fight with an adversary, struggle with a problem, argue with one's wife*: in such cases, one might imagine oneself and one's adversary proceeding together in the same movement, the same furious dance. But notice how this apparent confusion is clarified in the following example: in a game of bridge, North and South are playing with East and West. To make it clear who are partners and who are opponents, we say *North is playing with South, East is playing with West*, and *North and South are playing together against East and West.*

Other Relationships: Between, Among

337 X may stand or move between two objects, Y and Z, thus:

$$\text{Y.} \quad (\text{X} \quad \text{or} \quad \downarrow \quad \text{X}) \quad \text{.Z}$$

or *among more than two.*

Note *I can divide this money between you two* or *distribute it among* (or *amongst*) *you all*. In popular speech, *between* is often used for *more than two.* Even speakers consciously endeavouring to restrict *between* to two things only, would feel it unnatural to do so when discussing, for example, *the difference between various factors,* although in such a situation they might be thinking of the difference between only two factors at a time, i.e. between X and Y, and then between X (or Y) and Z.

Like, As

338 In comparing one thing with another, we may find that *X is like Y,* or *unlike* it. A distinction is made, and still insisted upon by grammarians, between the preposition *like,* which indicates a relationship between objects, and the conjunction *as* introducing a subordinate, finite clause e.g. *John walks just like his father,* but *He walks just as his father used to* (*walk*). Most grammarians would consider it 'incorrect' to use *like* in the second example, although it is becoming common among native speakers of English. Nor would traditional grammar classify *as* as a preposition—even in the phrase you have just read. Yet it is difficult not to consider *as* with the ·other little words in this chapter. However grammarians may classify *as,* the student will no doubt want to see the difference between, say, *He spoke to me like a father* (comparison) and *He wrote to me as my legal adviser* (in that role or capacity).

Freedom of Choice

339   One can arrive at a point on the map (*We arrived at the station five minutes early*), arrive on what one sees as a surface (*We arrived on the platform just as the train was coming in*), or arrive in a space (*We arrived in London late last night*). One can be *on a chair* or *in a chair*, according to whether the speaker has in mind the surface of the seat or the space contained by the seat, the back and the arms. One can be *in bed* on a cold night, or can rest *on the bed* on a hot afternoon (for *in bed v on the bed*, see **99**). One can drive *across London*, or *through it*, according to whether one sees it as a surface-area or a conglomeration of streets and buildings.

Influence of Latin and Greek

340   The Latin prepositions—*ab* (= from), *ad* (= to), *cum* (= with), *de* (= from), *ex*, *e* (= from, out of), and the Greek *sym* (= with)—absorbed into English words as prefixes, tend to attract the English prepositions which are supposed to be equivalent in meaning. Thus: *absent from*, *adhere to*, *communicate with*, *different from*, *exempt from*, *sympathise with*. With *different* there would appear to be a conflict between etymology, which requires the preposition *from*, and the tendencies in modern English which I am trying to trace in this chapter. Many native English-speakers, uninhibited by a strict grammatical teaching, point from one thing to another, and remark that *this is different to that*. That is natural and logical, even if it is incorrect by traditional rules. On the other hand, *depend on* (cp. *hang on*) is recognised as 'correct', although speakers of languages derived from Latin are being consistent etymologically when they say **depend from*. With words of this kind, be careful to observe what the object of the prefix is: for example, in *The dishonest cashier absconded with the cash*, *absconded* means 'go or hide away *from* somewhere', and in that example *with* is a straightforward usage as in **335**. Note, similarly, *appeal (to someone) for a donation*.

Mechanical Association

341   While the foregoing paragraphs in this chapter may have provided some form of systematisation for the English prepositions, a great many usages can only be mastered by mechanical association, especially where the idea of movement or position in space is very weak or absent altogether. I can offer no 'explanation' for such associations as *afraid of* (*nothing*), *believe in* (*miracles*), *suffer from* (*an illness*), *congratulate* (*you*) *on* (*your success*). The student must not be surprised if he finds that in some of these purely mechanical associations even native-English usage can be uncertain and conflicting. In any case, an important element in English grammatical usage is knowing what prepositions are used in verb patterns (see Chapter 7, **275**, especially SVO 2, SVOO 3 and 4 and SVOC 4 and 5), and in adjective patterns (**277–278**). Carefully noticing usage, copying out the verb or adjective together with a prepositional phrase attached to it, and noting the examples given in a good dictionary, are perhaps the only ways of establishing these associations, though I hope this chapter will have made many of them clearer.

Prepositions in Relative Clauses, and Questions

342　All the prepositions (except *during* and *since*[1]) can fit into the following patterns:

(*a*) *I am referring to the question of your debts.*
(*b*) *That is the question to which I am referring.*
(*c*) *That's the question I'm re'ferring to.*

(*b*) is more formal; and, in spoken English, sounds clumsy and unnatural; (*c*), more colloquial, though becoming increasingly acceptable in writing. In the interrogative, note

(*d*) *To what are you re'ferring?* (note as for (*b*)).
(*e*) *What are you re'ferring to?* (note as for (*c*)).

Adverbial Particles

343　The preposition separated from its object, as in **342**, must be distinguished from the adverbial particle, which indicates a movement or position in space or time without direct reference to an object. Most of the prepositions can be used as adverbial particles, but not all of them can be. Those that can be are shown below:

Preposition	Adverbial Particle
Walk across the street.	How can we get across?
I saw him coming along the road.	Come along.

[1] *During* and *since* are acceptable in patterns (*a*), (*b*) and (*d*), but not in (*c*) and (*e*). Example: *Since when have you been in charge? During which months does India have its heaviest rainfall?*

Preposition	Adverbial Particle
Who is that behind you?	Don't be left behind.
My cabin is below the main deck.	I'm going below.
I passed by your window.	Why pass by?
Go down the hill.	Go down.
Keep in front of me.	Keep in front.
Get in the car.	Get in.
Stay inside the house.	Stay inside.
Get off the bus.	Get off quickly.
Get on the bus.	Get on again.
Go out of the room.	Go out.
Stay outside the house.	Stay outside.
Jump over the gate.	Jump over.
Drive past the school.	Drive past.
Since New Year.	I haven't seen him since.
Get through the hole.	How can I get through?
Crawl under the rope.	Can you crawl under (*or* underneath)?
Run up the hill again.	Run up again.

Notice *run about*, i.e. 'run in various directions'; *about turn*, in marching, i.e. 'turn and go the opposite way'; and *turn round*, i.e. perform one of the movements illustrated in **317**. *Turn over* expresses the movement illustrated in **334**. This movement could make a complete circle and continue thus, as in *a log rolling over and over* or *saying the same thing over and over again*. In *the war is over* (i.e. ended) or in *I've finished my shopping and have two pounds over* (i.e. remaining), we are concerned with the termination of the movement in **334**. Note the special uses of *off* and *out*, in *set off* (i.e. off the starting-line, start on a journey) and *set out* (i.e. out of one's home or one's base, also at the beginning of a journey; *look out* (from one's base) and *point out*; *down*, in *turn down, breakdown*.

344 The adverbial particles thus express movement or positions in space and time similar to those expressed by the corresponding prepositions. The following are not used as adverbial particles: *to, at, from, towards, till, for, of, into, during, with, without, against*, though the nouns that follow can sometimes be omitted and understood, as in *Are you for the motion* (i.e. proposal in a debate), *or against?* Note also *come 'to* (recover from unconsciousness) and *go* or *do without* (something). On the other hand, there are two important particles with no corresponding prepositions, namely *away* and *back*, e.g. *Don't go away. Please come back.*

Adverb Particles with Other Meanings

345 In addition to the basic meanings given in **344**, *on*, *off*, *in*, *out* and *up* have the following special meanings:

On indicates movement forwards, continuity, e.g. *go on*, *keep on*, *lead on*, *play on*. A light or a tap can be *on* (or *off*).

In indicates collapse, as in *give in*: colloquial *done in* or *all in* (exhausted).

Off suggests departure, as in *set off* and *They're off* (i.e. have started, in a race). The departure may be very sudden, as in *The firework went off almost in my face*.

Out can suggest movement in any direction away from a starting point, as in *Set out* (= start), *Give out these papers* (i.e. hand one to everybody) and *The soldiers spread out* (i.e. moved away from one another). *Out* can also suggest disappearance, as in *Blow out the light. The fire is out. Burn out, die out*.

Up has three special meanings:

(*a*) it can serve as a means of arousing and encouraging, as in *hurry up!* (but *don't hurry*), *speak up* (i.e. speak more loudly, or don't be afraid to speak), *play up*, *keep up* (i.e. *don't go slowly*), *poke the fire up* (to make it burn more brightly).

(*b*) it can indicate stoppage, as in *give up* (i.e. surrender), *hold up* (i.e. delay), *the game is up* (it's no use continuing the struggle).

346 *Up* (in its third special meaning) and *out* are also often used to emphasise the completion of the act. Notice the difference in the ways *eat* is used in the following examples:

[9] Some people eat too much. (**S O**, as in **137**).
[10] Eat up your dinner! Finish it. (**I O**).
[11] You are eating too quickly. (**I U**, as in **137**).
[12] I am eating it all up. (**I U**).

We can imagine a mother saying [10] and [11] to a child, and the child replying with [12]. In *I eat* and *I am eating* we are concerned with the act as a whole, *I am eating* emphasising the action in progress. In *I eat up* and *I am eating up* we are concerned with the completion of the act, *eating up* emphasising the idea of being in the process of completing the act. Similarly, we have *I drink*, *I am drinking*, *I drink up*, *I am drinking up*.

Other examples of *up* used in this way are:

[13] We've saved up (money) to buy a house!

[14]   Look up this word in the dictionary.
[15]   Why not call up a few friends (on the telephone) and ask them round (to our house) for a party?

Save is also used without *up*, as in *Don't waste electricity. Save it!* *Up* could be omitted in example [13], but then the idea of having completed the saving would be lost. *Up* could not be omitted from examples [14] and [15].

347   *Out* is also used to indicate completion of the act as in

[16]   I've found out what is wrong with this machine.
[17]   May I point out where you have made a mistake?
[18]   I can't solve this problem. How did *you* work it out?

Out could perhaps be omitted from example [16], but not from [17] and [18].

Adverbial Particle + Preposition

348   It frequently happens, especially in spoken English, that direction and position are indicated by an adverbial particle (or even two particles) followed immediately by a preposition. Examples:

[19]   We walked on (*i.e. continued our journey*) to Rome.
[20]   I'm just going across to the grocer's (*i.e. across the road to . . .*); *or* over to the grocer's (*i.e. over the road*).
[21]   I'll come along (the road) to the station with you.
[22]   Go down (*i.e. downstairs*) to the kitchen.
[23]   John's gone off (*i.e. left the house*) to school.
[24]   He's gone up to the senior school now.
[25]   Can you help me get up onto the roof?
[26]   (*a*) Where's John?
       (*b*) He's up on the roof.
[27]   We must have something in reserve to fall back on.

Note the difference between *on to*, in example [19], and *onto* (**322**); and the difference between *up on* in example [26] and *upon* in **326.**

Phrasal Verbs

349   What are generally called 'phrasal verbs', i.e. constructions consisting of verbs plus the little words we have been discussing in this chapter, are very frequently used in English. In the main, these constructions are formed by the verb *be* or a simple verb expressing physical action—*come, go*; *put, take*; *give, get*; *do, make*; *let, keep*; *bring, send*; *stand, fall, sit*; *turn*; *break, tear, throw*; *walk, run,* *jump*—followed by a preposition or particle indicating direction or position.

350 The student should have no difficulty in understanding *Mr Smith is in, out, away, back. He has gone (or come) in, out, inside, outside, up, down. It's raining—put the chairs inside. It's stopped—take them out again. I've given away all my money. How can I get it back again? You'll have to do without. Please let me in—don't keep me out in the rain. Don't stop—keep on. I'll keep in front—you keep up with the rest of the party. Send my breakfast up to my room. Bring it back, I haven't finished. I'll send it round to your office. Stand up, stand outside. Don't fall down, don't fall over. Sit down, but sit up straight. Turn round, turn over. Thieves broke in. Fire broke out. Who's torn up my paper? Who's torn down the notice I put up on the board? Walk out quietly. The dish ran away with the spoon. Our dog ran along behind the car.*

351 These phrases tend to become fixed expressions with special meanings. Thus, in the morning I *wake up*, *get up* and am then *up* (i.e. out of bed). My bedroom is on the second floor: I am upstairs. I go downstairs, and am then *down*. I *put on* my hat and *go out*. The streets are crowded: I try to *get on* (i.e. make progress) but am *held up* (delayed) by the traffic. So I *make up* my mind to *go back* till the rush is *over*. That is simple enough, and the student can easily get into the habit of using such expressions. The meaning may not be so obvious, though it should now be understandable, in phrases like *Stand up to him, don't be afraid, fight back. I'll try, but don't feel up to it* (i.e. capable of it). *I'll stand up for you* (defend you), *I won't let you down* (I won't fail to support you). *I've given you my word and I won't go back on it. We'll see this through together* (will go through this experience, and finish it, together: cp. *Mr Britling Sees it Through*, by H. G. Wells). *We won't give up the struggle: if there are difficulties, we'll put up with them* (i.e. give up worrying about them, and stop or stay *with* them). To *put up* at a hotel for the night is to stop on one's journey and stay there.

352 What are generally called 'phrasal verbs' are of four main types:

1. *Verb + preposition*, or prepositional verb (see Chapter 7, **275**, SVO 2, and the note on SVO 2 in **276**). The meaning should by now be obvious in prepositional verbs like *laugh at, look for, talk about, write about*. For the meaning of *at*, see **304** (*b*) (iii); of *for*, see **308**;

of *about*, see **317**. The meaning is not so obvious in *idiomatic phrasal verbs* like *come across*, meaning 'find or meet by chance'. All constructions of this type are transitive, i.e. they must be followed by an object, and many of them can be put into the passive, as in *Have we dealt with this question before? Has it been dealt with already?* Note that the preposition, if monosyllabic, is unstressed, so that stress falls on the verb, not on the preposition, in *Has this been 'dealt with? What are you 'looking at?*

2. *Verb + adverbial particle* (see **275**, SV 1a and note on SV 1a in **276**). There are innumerable combinations with *break, come, get, keep, stand, fall, run, turn, walk* and the particles mentioned in **344** and **345**. The meaning of many of them, e.g. *come in*, needs no explanation: it is enough to say that in normal everyday English *come in* would occur more frequently than the more formal *enter*. The meaning of idiomatic phrasal verbs, like *give in* or *give up* (i.e. surrender) is less obvious, though in those cases *in* and *up* are simply used as in **345**. Constructions of this type are intransitive and do not occur in the passive. The particle is stressed.

3. *Verb + object + particle* (see **275**, SVO 1b and note on SVO 1b). This meaning is obvious in *Take this rubbish away, Take away this rubbish, Take it away* and in innumerable other expressions in which *put, take, get, give, do, make, let, keep, bring, send, turn, break, tear, throw* etc., i.e. transitive verbs expressing physical action, especially monosyllabic ones, are combined with *away, back* and other particles referring to direction. The meaning is not obvious in idiomatic phrasal verbs such as *make up*, in the sense of 'invent' (a story) or 'turn down', i.e. reject (a proposal). Whether used literally or metaphorically, all constructions on this pattern are transitive and can be put into the passive. (*This rubbish must be taken away.*) The particle is, again, stressed.

4. *Verb + particle + prepositional + object:* see **348**. Again, the particle is stressed, the preposition unstressed. The passive is sometimes found, as in the informal *This work must be got on with at once. This is not a situation that can be put up with easily.*

CHAPTER 10

Adverbials

353 The main problem with adverbials—single-word adverbs (e.g. *badly*, *often*) or adverbial phrases (*to Spain*)—is to know where to put them. There are numerous kinds of adverbial, but they have one thing in common: they do not normally stand between the verb and its object. Nor do they occur between the object and the particle in a phrasal verb (**352**, 3). Thus, *very well* and *strictly* are in their normal, proper positions in:

[1]   Eric speaks English very well.
[2]   They brought their children up strictly.

In *I don't like very much sugar*, *very much* is a quantifier (**51**) meaning 'a great amount of'. In *I don't like sugar very much*, the same phrase is an adverbial making the sentence mean 'My liking for sugar is not very great.'

354 Exceptionally, an adverb may separate verb and object; but there must be a good reason for making the exception, e.g. to avoid ambiguity, or because the object is a long noun phrase, or to produce a dramatic effect. Thus in

[3]   We must examine carefully the meanings of the words we use,

ambiguity would result if *carefully* were placed after *use* instead of after *examine*; and in

[4]   He opened, very slowly, the most amazing book I have ever seen,

the delay in introducing the object creates an atmosphere of suspense.

355 Adverbials are of two main types: first, there are those that form part of the structure of a sentence, being usually pronounced within its main intonation pattern, and called *adjuncts*; second, there are those that fall outside the sentence structure, are pronounced before the main intonation pattern begins or after it ends, or interrupt the intonation: these occur normally in a sentence that follows another sentence, and for that reason they are called *sentence adverbials*. This second type can itself be sub-divided. There are *disjuncts* (e.g. *perhaps*, *personally*) which, like the modals in their secondary function (**214**), allow the speaker to express a personal attitude towards the statement he is making; and *conjuncts* (e.g. *therefore*, *however*) which serve as logical links between one sentence or paragraph and another.

356 Occasionally, the same word may serve as adjunct in one sentence and disjunct in another. For example:

[5]　Nancy was not behaving naturally.
[6]　Naturally, I imagined she was feeling upset.
[7]　Peter did not behave properly.
[8]　Quite properly, he was punished for it.

In [5], *naturally* is an adjunct and the intonation pattern includes, and falls on, that word. In [6], *naturally* (*I imagined*) means 'it seemed to me natural': *naturally* has an intonation to itself, and is separated from the rest of the sentence by a comma. Similar comments could be made on *properly*. Example [6] could be re-arranged as follows:

[6a]　I imagined she was feeling upset, naturally.

or

[6b]　I imagined, naturally, she was feeling upset.

The commas in [6a] and [6b] are obligatory. The comma in [6a] marks the end of the main intonation pattern, while the commas in [6b] mark an interruption in the pattern. Similar comments would apply to the position of conjuncts and to the punctuation used with them.

357 The chief source of difficulty with adverbials is with adjuncts, which are of various kinds, as we shall see below. The most usual place for an adjunct is at the end of a sentence, after the obligatory elements in the sentence pattern. In the sentence *He makes watches*, all the elements, SVO (**273**), are obligatory, and an adjunct like *beautifully* will come at the end, to produce SVO A. The element A is structurally optional there, providing additional information. Notice that the sentence *He makes watches beautifully* answers the question '*How* does he make watches?' and that the emphasis in the answer falls on *beautifully*.

358 An adjunct can also occur in the middle of a sentence, as in

[9] He slowly opened that amazing book.

There, the sentence answers the question 'What exactly did he do?': *slowly* does not add information at the end but, rather, modifies the verb. The mid-position adverb is thus intimately connected with the verb, is almost a part of it, as though there were a verb *to slowly-open*. Fear of the grammarian's taboo on the 'split infinitive' as it is called, caused me to insert a hyphen between *slowly* and *open*. Yet *I want you to creep downstairs and to slowly open the front door* might sound perfectly natural in spoken English, whereas **He used to beautifully make watches* would sound as alien as **He speaks very well Russian*.

359 What was said in **358** is relevant to single-word adverbs of frequency, e.g. *always, frequently, generally, never, occasionally, often, rarely, seldom, sometimes, usually* (and *ever* in questions and the negative). These adverbs are closely associated with verbal aspect (see Chapter 5), insofar as they draw attention to a series of acts (S, in **137**). S O is exemplified in *I always go, I often go* etc.; and S U in *You're always tapping on the table*: indeed, *always* or *constantly*, is an essential factor in that particular example of S U. Similarly, single-word adverbs of degree (e.g. *almost, hardly, just,*[1] *nearly, quite,*[2] *scarcely*) that usually indicate the degree to which an act is completed (see **132** (*b*)), and adverbs of relative time (*already, just, lately, recently, soon, still, yet*), which are obviously aspects of time (**131**), are closely associated with the verb and are usually found in the mid-position in the sentence.

360 The mid-position can be defined with reference to the operator (**210**), the adverb coming immediately *after* the operator, as in

[10] You are always tapping. . . . I have often seen you doing it.
[11] He has never been seen again.

It will come immediately before a verb in the Simple Present or

---

[1] *Just* can be an adverb of degree, as in *I just passed my examination*, i.e. I obtained the minimum pass mark. It can also be an adverb of relative time, e.g. *I have just seen the results*, i.e. very recently. Or it can be a focusing adverb, as in *He just ran*, i.e. he did that and nothing else.

[2] *Quite* means 'moderately' before a 'gradable' adjective or adverb, e.g. *good, carefully*, but 'absolutely' before an 'ungradable' word, e.g. *right, perfectly*.

Simple Past (*I always go. He never went*); but if *do* as an operator is required, the mid-position adverb immediately follows it as before, as in

[12]   I do sometimes take you out for dinner, you know.

In an emphatic affirmative, especially in contradiction to a negative, the adverb can precede the operator, which is then strongly stressed:

[13]   A. You never go by bus these days.
       B. I beg your pardon. I always *do* go by bus.

361   In answer to a question that requires a definite or emphatic statement of frequency, a normally mid-position adverb can come at the end of the sentence, as in

[14]   A. How often do you go to see your dentist?
       B. I don't know exactly, but I go sometimes.

Frequently, *generally*, *occasionally*, *often* could replace *sometimes* in that example; and we can say *I've been there recently* (or *lately*), *I haven't been there yet*, *I'll go soon*. But *just* and *never* would not be found in final position, nor would the single-word adverbs of degree mentioned in **359**. Adverbs of frequency that can end a sentence can also come at the beginning, especially for contrast with something that has been said before: e.g.

[15]   I never miss my breakfast. Sometimes, it's true, I only have a piece of toast.

Never, like *hardly*, *scarcely*, *seldom* and *rarely* (indeed, like any other word implying a negative) could not begin a sentence without inversion of subject and verb:

[16]   Never (Seldom, Rarely) has there been such a spectacle.

(cp. *Only then* (i.e. not until then) *did I realise how serious the situation was*.) *Ever*, on the other hand, always occupies mid-position:

[17]   Have you ever/Did you ever/Do you ever put your foot on a snake?

Still and *yet* at the beginning of a sentence are usually conjuncts, the former meaning 'All the same', the latter 'Nevertheless'.

362   In the interrogative, the mid-position adverb follows operator

+ subject (example [17]). In the negative, it usually follows operator + *not*:

[18]   I haven't ever been there. We haven't often thought about it.

Nearly would fit into the pattern of [18] (*We haven't nearly finished*); but *almost* would not occur with a negative. Nor would *never, hardly, rarely, seldom, scarcely*, since they are all negative in meaning, and a double negative is unacceptable in English. *Sometimes* normally comes before the operator + *not* (e.g. *I sometimes don't go to bed till twelve.*). *Still* can come before or after *not*, but with a difference in meaning: *He's not still waiting* means that he has stopped waiting, while *He's still not waiting* means that he has not started waiting yet.

363 Adverbs of manner (as in **357**) typically come at the end of a sentence. However, what may appear to be adverbs of manner are not always easy to place. In examples [19] and [20], *legally* is an adverb of manner; and note that such an adverb can come before or after a passive construction. In example [21], the same word acts as a viewpoint adverb, and can occupy the same points as a disjunct or conjunct (**356**), with the same effect on intonation and punctuation:

[19]   We drew up the agreement legally.
[20]   It was legally drawn up (*or* drawn up legally).
[21]   Legally (*i.e. from a legal point of view*), the agreement is
         perfectly in order.

364 In **290** 4, we saw the difference between

[22]   (*a*) He kindly wrote to me

and

         (*b*) He wrote to me kindly.

In [22] (*a*) the adverb is closely linked with the subject: he was kind when he wrote to me. Note a similar difference between [23] and [24]:

[23]   I foolishly forgot to sign the letter.
[24]   In doing so, I acted absent-mindedly rather than foolishly.

365 A subtler distinction is found in [25] and [26]:

[25]   I remember that incident well. I well remember it.
[26]   You told that story well. *But not* *You well told it.

Well in an adverb of manner in [26], answering the question 'How did I tell that story?' Now an adverb of manner can modify a verb expressing action over which human control is possible, but not a verb of perception or cognition, like *see, hear, know, remember* (cp. **145–147**). *Well* in [25] does not answer the question 'How do you remember that incident?' but 'How clearly do you remember it?'. *Well* in [25] is therefore an adverb of degree. A similar distinction is seen in

[27]   I clearly remember the morning George came to school

and

[28]   He wrote all his notes very clearly.

366   Adverbs of time and position normally come at the end of the sentence. They can also be placed at the beginning, for emphasis, to set the scene in time or place, or for contrast with a previous statement. Adverbs of direction are usually found only at the end. However, if place (position or direction) and time occur in the same sentence, place normally precedes time. In both, place and time, more precise details are given before more general information. Thus:

[29]   Columbus discovered America in the fifteenth century.
[30]   He landed on the 12th of October 1492 (*or* on October the 12th, 1492).
[31]   Early in 1493, he returned to Spain (*but not* *To Spain he returned early in 1493).
[32]   He died at Valladolid in Spain in May 1506.
[33]   Throughout Latin America, October 12th is an annual holiday.

367   *Only* (meaning 'that and nothing else'), *even* (meaning 'that in addition to everything else') and *also* (meaning 'in addition to what has been mentioned already'), all focus attention on one particular element in a sentence. Uncertainty may arise, at least in writing, if the adverb is not placed as closely as possible to the element on which attention is meant to be focused. This uncertainty is less likely in spoken English, where the element concerned can be pronounced with stress and on a higher pitch than the rest of the sentence. Thus, though the speaker's precise meaning in *We can only lend these books to members of the library* may be conveyed quite clearly in speech, in print that sentence focuses attention on *lend* (and might suggest, for example, that the books cannot be sold). *Only these books* would high-light *these books,* while *only* after *library* would high-light *members of the library*. Similar comments would apply to *even* and *also*.

368   *Very* is an intensifier and can modify adjectives and adverbs provided they are gradable: thus *very good*, *very carefully* but not **very unique*, **very perfectly*. *Very* can be used with certain participal adjectives, i.e. *-ing* and *-ed* forms, e.g. *very interesting*, *very tired*. But only those *-ing* and *-ed* forms that have been fully established as adjectives can safely be modified by *very*; and in many cases other intensifiers must be used. Even with *interesting*, 'careful' speakers might feel *extremely* or *highly interesting* to be more appropriate. Note that *highly* tends to be used with words suggesting a good quality, while *utterly* frequently occurs with words suggesting the reverse, as in *utterly boring*. *Deeply* is often used with participal adjectives referring to feelings and emotions, as in *deeply disappointed*, *deeply hurt*; but *badly* or *seriously hurt* physically. Other examples are *completely forgotten*, *fully insured*, *thoroughly worn out* and *widely known*.

CHAPTER 11

When to Use That, What, Who, Which, Whether

That

369 (*a*) *That*, rhyming with *hat*, is a determiner—or, more precisely, a demonstrative, in *What is that (thing)?* It can be used as a substitute for a noun phrase, as in

[1]　The population of China is much greater than that of Japan.

(*b*) With a weak vowel in fluent speech like the unstressed vowel in *alone*, *that* is a subordinating conjunction introducing a *that*-clause: see **275,** SVO 11. It can be omitted in a short simple sentence, especially in fluent everyday speech, but only if the *that*-clause follows the verb of which it is an object. It is obligatory in a more complex sentence and if the *that*-clause begins the sentence, as in

[2]　That he was innocent has been proved beyond doubt.
[3]　That he was guilty of any crime, we cannot believe.

The *that*-clause acts as subject of *has been proved* in example [2], which could be re-worded, more idiomatically, as *It has been proved beyond doubt that he was innocent*. In example [3], the *that*-clause is object of *cannot believe*: intonation rises on *crime* and falls on *believe*. Contrast example [3] with

[4]　He was completely innocent, I believe.

There, *He was completely innocent* is an independent main clause; intonation falls on *innocent*; *that* cannot be included; and *I believe* is a comment clause.

(*c*) *That*, again with a weak vowel in fluent speech, is used as a relative pronoun, with either a personal or a non-personal antecedent, but (preferably) only in a restrictive relative clause (see **46,** section 30). It can therefore replace *who*, *whom* or *which*, it is preferred to *which* after an indefinite pronoun such as *all* or *everything*; but it cannot be used immediately after a preposition. It can be omitted if the relative pronoun would be object in the relative clause (e.g. *A man I know. The house I bought.*)

What

370   (*a*) *What* is a question-word, modifying a noun or acting as a pronoun, as in *What* (*thing*) *is that? What does this mean?* It refers to something non-personal.

(*b*) It can introduce an indirect question, as in *I don't know what this means?* i.e. I don't know the answer to the question *What does this mean?*

(*c*) It has a different function in

[5]   I've found what I want.
[6]   What I want is a long envelope.

In [5] and [6], *what I want* is not an indirect question, but a nominal relative clause, which could be expanded to *I want something, and that something is a long envelope*: in other words, to *The thing that I want is a long envelope.*

Whatever, etc.

371   The distinction between *what* and *whatever* is similar to that between *some* and *any*. Thus *Take what you want* means 'Take something that you want—take that particular but unspecified thing.' *Take whatever you want* means 'Take anything: it doesn't matter what it is: the choice is completely open to you'. A similar distinction can be made between *which* and *whichever*, *when* and *whenever*, *where* and *wherever*, *how* and *however*, *who* and *whoever*: but see **372**.

Who, Whoever

372   (*a*) *Who* is a question-word, used only as a pronoun, e.g. *Who is that?* It refers to a person, though sometimes also to domestic pets.

(*b*) It can introduce an indirect question, as in *I don't know who that was?*

(*c*) *Who* cannot be used like *what* in **370** examples [5] and [6]. In a nominal relative clause one would have to use *whoever*:

[7]   Take me to whoever is in charge of this establishment.
[8]   Whoever telephoned you has left the office now.

i.e. the person who is in charge, who telephoned.

(*d*) *Who* can replace *that* as a relative pronoun (see **369** (*c*)), but only when the antecedent is personal. It is the normal relative pronoun to use with a personal antecedent, in a *non*-restrictive relative clause (**46**, section 30, example [28]). *Who* (or *whom*), with a personal antecedent in a non-restrictive clause, cannot be omitted when the relative pronoun is in the objective case.

Whom, Whose

373   (*a*) *Whom* occurs, instead of *who*, in formal English when the question-word or relative pronoun is in the objective case: it would sound pedantic in everyday speech. However, it is obligatory in any style immediately after a preposition.

(*b*) *Whose*, as noun-modifier or as pronoun, e.g. *Whose* (*book*) *is this?* asks that the possessor be named.

(*c*) *Whose* is used as a relative pronoun in the genitive case, in either a restrictive or non-restrictive relative clause. It is certainly used when the antecedent is personal, and often used, rather than *of which*, with a non-personal antecedent.

Which

374   (*a*) *Which* is a question-word, modifying a noun or as a pronoun: it replaces *what* in this capacity when choice is specifically restricted, and it can refer (unlike *what* and *who*) both to animate and inanimate objects, e.g. *Which of these four things* (*or persons*) *did you see?*

(*b*) *Which*, as well as *that*, is used as a relative pronoun when the antecedent is non-personal, though *that* is preferred after an indefinite pronoun (see **369** (*c*)). In a *non*-restrictive relative clause, *which* is preferred to *that;* it cannot be omitted when the relative pronoun is in the objective case.

Whether

375   Either *if* or *whether* is an acceptable introduction to an indirect *Yes/No question*, as in **275**, SVO 13. In that case, *whether* may possibly suggest more doubt about an affirmative answer. But only *whether* is used (*a*) if the indirect question begins the sentence (*Whether he was ever found again is not known*) or (*b*) after a preposition (*My answer depends on whether. . . .*).

Questions beginning with What, Who, etc.

376   (*a*) Questions beginning with *what*, *who*, *whose* and *which*, in which the target is the subject of the sentences, do not require inversion of subject and auxiliary as in **210**, 2 and 3, thus:

Statement	Question	Answer
Something floats on water	What floats on water?	Wood does
Somebody broke the window	Who broke the window?	Jack did
Somebody's paper is missing	Whose (paper) is missing?	Mine is
One of these coats is yours	Which (coat) is yours?	That (one) is

(*b*) Questions in which the target is not the subject of the sentence, require first the *wh* – word, then the interrogative form as in **210**, 2 and 3:

Target	Question	(*Short*) Answer
Direct Object	What are you reading?	A book
Direct Object	What does 'halt' mean?	Stop
Indirect Object	To whom did you (send) the letter? (*formal*)	The Manager
Indirect Object	Who did you send the letter to? (*informal*)	The Manager
Complement	What is your name?	(My name is) X
Complement	What is your nationality?	(I'm) Swiss
Complement	How are you today?	(I'm) very well
Complement	What is the weather like?	(It's) rather cold
Adverb of place	Where does your father work?	In an office
Adverb of time	When were you born?	In 1965
Adverb of frequency	How often do you weigh yourself?	Once a week
Reason	Why didn't you stop?	Because . . . . .

CHAPTER 12

Functions and Notions

377 By 'function' I here refer to the purposes for which a grammatical construction is used in normal interpersonal communication: thus, the function of the construction *Might I use your telephone?* is to make a polite request. By 'notion' I refer to an abstraction such as 'request'. To describe the function of a grammatical construction, one must generally resort to notions which can usually only be labelled by abstract nouns. While the English grammatical system can be relatively easily described, e.g. by reference to combinations of Noun Phrases and Verb Phrases, to an analysis of such phrases and to the kind of sentence patterns outlined in Chapter 7 of this book, it is much more difficult to arrange abstract notions in a system. The Synopsis of Categories used by Roget in his famous *Thesaurus* is too complex for the purposes of this present chapter. I shall therefore give an alphabetical list of one hundred notions—the number has been chosen arbitrarily and could be far greater—and under each entry will provide examples of grammatical constructions by which the functions associated with the entry are frequently performed.

378 It will be seen that examples—for instance, of *advice, apology, blame, command, congratulations, denial, insistence, suggestion, warning*—are generally given below in direct speech, though in a style that would also be suitable for writing. The words *advise, apologise*, etc. are often not used in the examples at all. However, those words would be used very appropriately in indirect speech, as in [5] (*g*), [8] (*e*), [10] (*e*), [13] (*c*), [17] (*f*), [24] (*c*).

[1] Ability

    (*a*) John has ability (*in general*) but is inclined to be lazy.
    (*b*) He has the ability to (*or simply* he can) do much better.
    (*c*) You can speak English quite (*moderately*) well (see **359** footnote).
    (*d*) You will be able to speak fluently in a year's time.

Note that example (*c*) refers to present time only. However, we can say:

(*e*) If you can speak fluently in a year's time, you can go to a higher class.

(*f*) Your brother could write English very well when he was your age.

(*g*) You told me you could understand everything I said.

(*h*) Jack was able to pass his driving test the first time.

Note that *could* serves as the past for *can* (*i*) when reference is made to more than one attempt (as in (*f*)); but not as in (*h*) and (*ii*) in indirect speech. *Could* is not used to refer to one successful attempt; see (*h*). However, *I couldn't* as in (*i*), means that I did not have the ability, so I failed, although I made only one attempt:

(*i*) I took the driving test once, but I couldn't pass it.

Could have + *-ed* refers to either ability or permission not used in the past.

(*j*) You could have passed the examination if you had not been so nervous.

(*k*) I didn't take the test as I knew I couldn't have passed it.

(*l*) You could have borrowed my car—I said I would let you use it.

Note that *be able* (or *unable*) can supply all the missing parts of the 'defective verb' *can:*

(*m*) We have been able (or unable) to solve the problem.

(*n*) You must be able to understand spoken English.

[2]   Acceptance

(*a*) I'd be delighted to dine with you on Thursday. Thank you so much. (informal)

(*b*) Mr and Mrs D. A. Smith thank Dr and Mrs Robert Thompson for their kind invitation to dinner on Thursday, June 14th and have much pleasure in accepting.

[3]   Achievement

(*a*) At last we were able to reach the summit. We succeeded in reaching it at last (as in [1] (*h*) above).

Achievement can be expressed by the non-progressive form of the verb, when the progressive form suggests only an attempt at achievement.

(*b*) Roger climbed to the summit before sunset, but Taylor was still climbing when night fell.

[4]   Acknowledgement

(*a*) Thank you for your letter of May 27th (normal in correspondence).

(*b*) I hereby acknowledge receipt of your cheque for £1,000 (more formal).

(*c*) I am grateful (*or* indebted) to Mary Coulson for her assistance in compiling the index to this book.

[5]   Advice

(*a*) Drive carefully. Don't go too fast. You'd better fasten your seat belt.

(*b*) Slow down and take care when you come to the cross-roads.

(*c*) You should (*or* ought to) stop smoking; and you shouldn't (*or* oughtn't to) eat so much.

(*d*) I would cut down on smoking, or stop it entirely if I were you.

(*e*) I think you must see a doctor about that cough of yours.

(*f*) You would be well advised to consult a lawyer (more formal).

(*g*) You advised me to consult a lawyer.

[6]   Age

(*a*) *A* How old are you? (informal) *B* I'm sixteen (years old)

(*b*) *A* What is your (present) age? (an official question)
   B (My age is) sixteen

(*c*) *A* How old is that tree? *B* It is over two hundred years old.

Note that *years old* can be omitted in (*a*) which refers to a human being, but not in (*c*), i.e. where reference is made to something impersonal.

[7]   Agency

(*a*) We'll get the tickets (here *we* are the agents or actors).

(*b*) We'll get a cool reception, I'm afraid (here the agent is not mentioned).

(*c*) Quick! Mary has been bitten by a poisonous snake.

After a verb in the passive, a prepositional phrase beginning with *by* can refer to the agent; but such a phrase is necessary only when mention of the agent is relevant: it is not relevant in:

(*d*) Rome was not built in a day.

[8]   Agreement

(*a*) *A* This is the best way to take.
   B Yes, I think it is (*or* I agree *or* You're right *or* All right, let's take it).

(*b*) *A* That's Lucy Lockheart over there.

     B So it is (I agree that it is).

(*c*) I quite agree (i.e. I entirely agree) with you, with everything you say.

(*d*) You two are always quarrelling. Can't you agree about anything?

(*e*) We agree to (or accept) your general proposal. Now we must agree on the details.

(*f*) The Foreign Ministers failed to reach complete agreement.

(*g*) You agreed to come this way, didn't you? (see [8] (*a*) above).

[9] Anxiety

(*a*) I'm very worried about Jane. I don't think she is well enough to travel.

(*b*) I know you are anxious to hear about your daughter; but I can relieve your anxiety by assuring you that all of the passengers are safe and well.

[10] Apology

(*a*) I'm very sorry to be so late. I'm sorry I was so rude (informal).

(*b*) I do apologise for coming so late (more effusive).

(*c*) Mr D. A. Smith regrets that he will be unable to attend the meeting on June 14th.

(*d*) Miss Lucy Lockheart thanks Mr and Mrs D. A. Smith for their kind invitation to supper on July 5th, but very much regrets that she has a prior engagement for that evening.

(*e*) He apologised for arriving late and for being so rude (see [10] (*a*) above).

[11] Arrangements

(*a*) We've arranged to go to Paris next week and arranged for Mary to come too.

(*b*) So we're going to Paris and Mary is coming too (arrangements have been made).

[12] Beginning of an action or state

(*a*) We're arriving. Wake up—we're landing (i.e. beginning to arrive, to land).

(*b*) I'm forgetting my German (i.e. beginning to forget it).

(*c*) I hated this place at first, but now I'm coming (beginning) to like it.

[13]   Blame

(*a*) It was my fault entirely. I am (entirely) to blame for the accident.

(*b*) No one is to blame (to be blamed) but myself.

(*c*) He blamed himself entirely for the accident.

[14]   Cause and Effect

(*a*) This noise makes me nervous. It makes me forget what I wanted to say.

(*b*) The blow knocked him unconscious. It rendered him speechless.

(*c*) The fire was caused by a burning cigarette end.

[15]   Certainty

(*a*) It is certain (or sure) to rain (i.e. I, the speaker, am certain that it will rain).

(*b*) They are certain (or sure) to win (the speaker is certain that they will).

(*c*) They are certain (or sure) of winning (they themselves are certain that they will).

(*d*) This must be the right road, surely (the speaker feels certain that it is).

[16]   Change of State

(*a*) Wilson became President. Edison soon became famous.

(*b*) We are all growing older—and I hope, wiser.

(*c*) Father is going bald. His hair, such as it is, is turning grey.

(*d*) This milk has gone (or turned) sour, and the meat has gone bad.

(*e*) The little Princess turned into a beautiful butterfly.

(*f*) The wicked knight turned traitor.

[17]   Commands or Orders

(*a*) Leave this house at once. Don't ever come back.

(*b*) You must do this work again. It is not good enough.

(*c*) Will you sit down and be quiet! Sit down, will you!

(*d*) You will all stay here till I return. Is that clear?

(*e*) You are to report to me at 4 o'clock every afternoon.

(*f*) He ordered them to report at 4 o'clock every afternoon.

[18]   Comparisons

(*a*) Dick is as old as I am, but he is two years younger than Frank (is).

(*b*) Therefore, Frank is not as (*or* so) young as Dick (is).

(*c*) He is taller than I am (*or* than me). I'm shorter than him (informal).

(*d*) This house is much (*or* far) more expensive than the one we lived in before.

(*e*) Our old house was very much less expensive. It was not nearly as (*or* so) expensive as this one (is).

(*f*) Compared with our old house, this one is much brighter. By (*or* in) comparison with our present house, our former one was dark and gloomy.

(*g*) Murray's work is superior to Norton's. Norton's, I think, is definitely inferior.

[19] Concession
(*a*) John may be clever—I admit that—but he is very careless.

(*b*) Although John is clever, he has never won a prize yet.

(*c*) However hard he tries, he always makes too many little mistakes.

[20] Congratulations
(*a*) Well done. Splendid. That was excellent.

(*b*) Congratulations on your success. You must be very pleased.

(*c*) May I offer you my sincere congratulations on your new appointment? (rather formal, written style).

[21] Consequence (see also Cause and Effect)
(*a*) Please keep this gate shut, or the cattle will stray.

(*b*) Some fool left the gate open and all the cows have got out.

(*c*) If you touch that wire, you'll get a nasty shock.

(*d*) No agreement was reached, so the meeting was adjourned.

(*e*) Chemical waste from a factory polluted the river. Consequently, all the fish died.

[22] Contrast
(*a*) Robert was completely different from Thomas.

(*b*) Whereas Robert was patient and always thoughtful of others, Thomas, in contrast, was hasty and inconsiderate.

[23] Degree
(*a*) Some of the work you have given me is very bad.

(*b*) Some is not so bad but not (nearly) good enough.

(*c*) Some is just good enough, but could be (much) better.

(*d*) Some is fairly good; some quite (i.e. moderately) good.

(*e*) The rest is very good indeed, but none of it is quite (i.e. 100%) perfect yet.

[24]   Denial

(*a*) *A*   Look what you've done to my car!

B   But I̲ did not do that. I never came into contact with your car a̲t all.

(*b*) *A*   I'm sorry, but you backed right into it when you were parking.

B   Excuse me, but that isn't so. I never touched your car sir.

(*c*) *B* denied hitting (or having hit) *A*'s car.

[25]   Determination

(*a*) I will finish this job even if it kills me. I won't give up.

(*b*) You will finish this job if it takes you all night: I'm determined you will.

(*c*) I'm going to stay here till this job is finished.

(*d*) I'm (absolutely) determined on seeing this work done well.

[26]   Dimensions

(*a*) *A*   How long (*or* wide *or* high) is this room?

B   It is six metres long, 3 metres wide and about 3 metres high.

(*b*) *A*   What is the length (width, height) of this room?

B   It is six metres in length, 3 metres in width and about 3 metres in height.

(*c*) This river is only two metres deep. Its depth is two metres exactly.

(*d*) *A*   How big is Africa? What is its total area?

B   Its total area is 11,500,000 square miles.

(*e*) A point has no dimension, a line has one, namely length; a surface or plane has two—either length and width, or length and height; a space or volume has three dimensions—length, width and height.

(*f*) A man may be tall or short, fat or thin. His fingers may be thin or thick.

(*g*) A building, a tree or a mountain may be tall (*or* high); or may be comparatively low.

[27]   Distance

(*a*) *A*   How far is it (from X) to Y? Is it as much as a hundred kilometres?

B It is quite a long way—quite far, in fact (note: avoid *it is far*). But it is not far from X to V.

(*b*) We cannot reach Rome today. It's too far (away).

[28] Doubt

(*a*) I doubt whether (*or* if) we shall get home by 7. I doubt it very much.

(*b*) I think it is most unlikely that we shall be home by 7.

(*c*) Don't worry. I don't doubt that we shall be there in time.

(*d*) I have no doubt about it. No doubt we shall have to hurry, though.

[29] Duration

(*a*) We have been living here for twenty years (emphasis on the duration of the period). c.p. We have lived here for twenty years (emphasis on the total achievement).

(*b*) We have been in this house since 1968 (i.e. during a period beginning in 1968).

(*c*) We shall be away for six weeks.

(*d*) I am staying in Brighton for a fortnight (i.e. two weeks from now).

(*e*) My parents lived in Australia for twenty years, till 1960 (i.e. during a period of twenty years ending in 1960).

(*f*) People kept coughing during the lecture (i.e. throughout a certain period).

(*g*) We shall wait here till 8 o'clock (i.e. our waiting will continue throughout a period, ending then).

(*h*) We shall not leave till 8 o'clock (i.e. our not-leaving will continue throughout a period ending then).

(*i*) The storm lasted (for) three days.

(*j*) It was raining continuously all that time (emphasis on duration of the rain).

[30] Emphasis

(*a*) I do want to succeed. I have tried. (stress the operator) **210** 5.

(*b*) I do *not* want to see that man again (stress on *not* in its uncontracted form) **207**.

(*c*) I can carry that suitcase. Heavy trunks I can't take (abnormal word order for emphasis).

(*d*) It was Jones who telephoned: I didn't (cleft sentence to emphasize *Jones*).

(*e*) What you saw was a shooting star (form of cleft sentence to emphasize *shooting star*).

(*f*) I gave it to *him*, not to her (stressed *him* for emphasis).

[31]   Excuse

(*a*) I'm sorry I'm late, but I missed the bus (it was therefore my fault).

(*b*) I'm sorry to be late, but the usual bus wasn't running (the bus was to blame).

(*c*) Don't make excuses; you must be punctual in future.

[32]   Existence

(*a*) There are millions of stars in the sky.

(*b*) Thousands of different kinds of gum tree are to be found in Australia.

[33]   Frequency

(*a*) I do *yoga* exercises for twenty minutes every morning.

(*b*) I have been to the theatre several times since I came here.

(*c*) We often (*or* sometimes *or* usually *or* never) go into town these days.

For other examples, and position of adverbials of frequency, see **359–362.**

[34]   General

(*a*) Cats are domestic animals (*cats* in general).

(*b*) Silver is a precious metal (*silver* in general).

(*c*) Frenchmen (*or* The French) drink wine (see **96**).

[35]   Habit

(*a*) We always go into the country on Sundays (our usual habit).

(*b*) I used to ride a bicycle, but now I drive a car (*used to* referring to past habit).

(*c*) That boy next door is always playing his hi-fi (constant, usually annoying, habit).

(*d*) Grandfather will sit watching television for hours (present habit, started in the past).

(*e*) My father would never let me watch television. (past habit).

(*f*) Do shut that door! You will leave it open (stressed will, indicating annoying habit).

[36]   Hesitation

(*a*) Excuse me, but might I ask you a personal question? (I hesitate to ask).

(*b*) I was wondering whether you would care to come out with me (I hesitate to ask).

(*c*) I'm thinking of buying myself a new suit (I haven't made up my mind yet).

[37] Impossibility

(*a*) This can't be the right road, surely (it is impossible for it to be so).

(*b*) There's no way of moving this rock.

[38] Insistence

(*a*) I <u>will</u> have silence (stressed <u>will</u> meaning 'I insist on it').

(*b*) Father <u>will</u> wear that same <u>old</u> jacket (stressed <u>will</u> meaning 'He insists on <u>it</u>').

(*c*) You must stay for supper. I insist.

[39] Instrument

(*a*) You can only open that door with a special key (*with* phrase indicating instrument).

(*b*) Only a special key will open that door (here the subject of the sentence refers to the instrument).

[40] Intention

(*a*) I will come and see you tomorrow (*will* indicating the speaker's intention).

(*b*) I'm going to stay in bed today (*be going to* indicating intention informally).

(*c*) I intend to wait (*or* I intend waiting) until you have written that letter.

[41] Invitation

(*a*) Will you come in? (rising intonation). Do come in. Come in, won't you?

(*b*) Would you like (*or* care) to come in? (very polite).

(*c*) Would you be free to have dinner with us on Friday? (informal).

(*d*) Mr and Mrs D. A. Smith request the pleasure of the company of Mr and Mrs R. T. Taylor on Friday, May 12th, at 8 p.m. (formal, written).

[42] Likelihood (or probability)

(*a*) We'll probably have some rain soon.

(*b*) It looks like rain (i.e. it looks as if (*or* though) it is going to rain).

(*c*) You'd better take an umbrella. It's quite likely to rain.

(*d*) I dare say you're right. It's quite probable.

(*e*) Mind this step. You'll slip if you're not careful.

[43] Location (see 26)

(*a*) We'll stop at this point.

(*b*) My parents live at Number 10, North Road.

(*c*) They live in a village in Yorkshire, in the north of England (in that area).

(*d*) Do people live on the moon? (i.e. on its surface).

(*e*) My hand is open. See: there is nothing on my hand at all (i.e. on that surface).

(*f*) Now it is closed. Is there anything in it now? (i.e. in that space).

[44] Manner

(*a*) He spoke very quietly, as if he did not wish to be overheard.

(*b*) James writes exactly like you. He forms each letter carefully, as you do.

(*c*) Muriel writes as if she were left-handed (but she isn't).

[45] Means (which explain how a certain operation can be, or was, performed)

(*a*) You can only open this lock by turning the key twice to the left.

(*b*) The Incas moved the massive stones into position by means of levers.

(*c*) Big Ben was dragged over Westminster Bridge by sixteen white horses.

[46] Method

(*a*) In these days, foreign languages are first taught orally (by the oral method).

(*b*) You can pay your bill by cash, cheque or credit card (by any of those ways).

(*c*) Food can be preserved in various ways e.g. drying it, freezing it, etc.

[47] Motion (compare this with **Location**)

(*a*) Trains on the Trans-Siberian Railway run from Vladivostok to Moscow.

(*b*) The trains go through tunnels, over bridges and along the south side of Lake Baikal.

(*c*) We got onto the train at Manchouli and went straight into our compartment.

(*d*) For two or three days, we travelled across a vast plain, then over the Ural Mountains.

[48] Necessity

(*a*) We must all eat in order to keep alive.

(*b*) You will have to take more exercise if you want to lose weight.

(*c*) Increasing blindness compelled Milton to stop reading altogether.

(*d*) It is not necessary (*or* there is no necessity) for you to come here every day.

(*e*) You needn't (*or* don't have to) come every day. There's no need to.

[49] Negation

(*a*) I did not say a word about it to anybody.

(*b*) In other words, I spoke to nobody about it.

(*c*) We have never seen such a magnificent spectacle.

(*d*) Never have we seen such a magnificent spectacle (more rhetorical than (*c*)).

(*e*) He answered without any hesitation and with no sign of nervousness.

(*f*) He denied taking (*or* having taken) any of the drug.

[50] Non-fact

(*a*) Hurry up. It's time you were in bed (past tense indicating non-fact).

(*b*) I'd rather you didn't leave me here all alone (past tense indicating non-fact).

(*c*) I wish you were tall (but you're not) (past tense indicating non-fact).

(*d*) If you had been listening, you would have heard the news (but you weren't listening).

[51] Objection

(*a*) I am sorry, Mr Chairman, but I cannot agree to that proposal.

(*b*) I do wish you wouldn't smoke in my office. I can't bear the smell.

(*c*) Does anyone mind if I turn on the television? (would anyone object?)

[52] Obligation

(*a*) I have to see the Director at ten o'clock.

(*b*) (I'm sorry to hear your mother is ill.) Of course you must go and see her.

(*c*) All books borrowed from the Library are to be returned by March 31st.

(*d*) I have done you an injustice and I owe you an apology.

(*e*) You are not obliged to say anything now.

(*f*) However, it is your duty to answer whatever questions the police put to you later.

[53]   Offer

(*a*) Will you have a drink? What will you have? (informal)

(*b*) Would you like something to drink? (slightly more formal).

(*c*) Please let me get you something to drink (slightly more formal).

(*d*) Can (*or* May) I offer you something to drink? (slightly more formal).

(*e*) Would you like to borrow my umbrella?

(*f*) A I'll pay £75 for that in cash.
    B £75? I've already turned down two better offers than that.

[54]   Orders (see command)

[55]   Particular (c.p. General)

(*a*) The cats were making an awful noise last night.

(*b*) Oh no! Burglars have taken all the silver.

(*c*) The Frenchmen spoke remarkably good English, didn't they?

[56]   Pardon

(*a*) I beg your pardon. I didn't mean to push you.

(*b*) I beg your pardon. Would you mind saying that again more slowly?

(*c*) I will forgive you (*or* let you off) this time; but don't do it again.

[57]   Permission (see also Requests)

(*a*) You can go now. There's no need to stay any longer.

(*b*) You may borrow this book if you promise to bring it back tomorrow.

(*c*) The Librarian said I might borrow this book.

(*d*) You are allowed to borrow any of the books except those in the Reference section.

(*e*) Smoking is permitted only on the top deck of the bus (formal).

[58]   Place (see Location)

[59]   Plans

(*a*) I'm going to meet a friend in town this morning and won't be back until five.

(*b*) I'm catching the nine o'clock train and taking a taxi to his hotel.

(*c*) I'm sorry I can't manage Thursday; I have meetings all day.

(*d*) *A* What are your plans for the summer?

    B We've arranged to spend two weeks in Greece and have a few days in Italy on the way. We leave on July 1st.

(*e*) These old houses are to be demolished next year and those trees are to come down.

[60] Possibility

(*a*) *A* Is there any way of stopping that door banging?

    B Yes, I'm sure it can be done. I'll put a spring on it.

(*b*) *A* I wonder why Miller isn't here today. Perhaps he's ill.

    B Yes he may be.

(*c*) I may be home very late this evening. Don't wait up for me.

(*d*) Why not telephone Miller's house? He might be ill (weaker possibility than *may be*).

(*e*) I might be home very late this evening, but I'll 'phone and let you know.

(*f*) Miller may have had an accident (it is possible that he had or has had, an accident).

(*g*) I agree he might have (had an accident), but surely we would have heard by now.

(*h*) Don't touch these thorns. They can be very painful.

[61] Prediction

(*a*) It will be my birthday on Saturday (certain prediction)

(*b*) Charles is going to be our spokesman (certain prediction).

(*c*) Solar Charge will win Thursday's race easily (a forecast that may prove wrong).

(*d*) It is going to be a fine day tomorrow (a forecast that may prove wrong).

(*e*) Solar Charge is certain to win (the speaker feels certain, but he may be wrong).

(*f*) William is certain of passing his test (William feels confident, but may be wrong).

[62] Preference

(*a*) What would you like, tea or coffee?

(*b*) I'd rather have coffee, black, please.

(*c*) *A* Shall we go for a swim?

    B I'd sooner go for a walk.

[63]   Probability (see **Likelihood**)

[64]   Prohibition

(*a*) Don't walk on the grass.

(*b*) No admittance except on business. Keep out.

(*c*) No Smoking. No Parking. No waiting between 8 am and 6 pm.

(*d*) No trespassers. Camping prohibited.

(*e*) I'm sorry, sir, but smoking is not permitted in the dining-room of this club.

(*f*) Does that mean I must put out my cigarette?

[65]   Promise

(*a*) I'll be home early this evening, dear, and take you out to dinner.

(*b*) I'll buy you a watch for your birthday.

(*c*) Don't worry. I'll pay you in full at the end of this month.

(*d*) It's all right. You shall have your money as soon as I get this month's pay.

(*e*) You will be promoted next year, provided your work is satisfactory.

[66]   Proposal

(*a*) I move (i.e. propose) that Elsworth's tender (i.e. price quoted for work to be done) be accepted.

(*b*) And I second (i.e. support) that proposal. I think we should accept it without delay.

(*c*) Will you marry me, darling? (a traditional proposal of marriage).

[67]   Purpose

(*a*) The speaker stopped to have a drink of water (that was his purpose in stopping).

(*b*) Open the window to let some of the smoke out.

(*c*) 'I pause for a reply.' (that is why I pause).

(*d*) The speaker paused so as to allow his audience to reply.

(*e*) The police closed the gates in order to prevent overcrowding.

(*f*) They closed the gates so that the people in front of the crowd should not be trampled on.

(*g*) 'We are closing the gates as a safety-measure, sir. We'll open them again to allow others to enter as soon as the way is clear.'

[68]   Quality

(*a*) *A* I want some material for a suit. Is this the best you have?

    B Oh no! That is not a good quality, rather poor in fact. We're selling it cheap.

(*b*) *A* Well, could you show me something better, please?

    B Yes, sir. Now this, is very fine quality—an excellent material.

[69] Quantity

(*a*) *A* How much bread have we left?

    B Not much, very little in fact.

(*b*) *A* How much water is there?

    B Quite a lot, plenty I think. Any amount.

(*c*) *A* How many eggs have we got?

    B Oh, a large number. Too many, I think.

(*d*) *A* Are there any apples?

    B A few. No, those are potatoes. Very few apples, I'm afraid.

(*e*) *A* How much of this medicine should I take?

    B No more than the prescribed quantity. One spoonful, three times a day.

[70] Reason

(*a*) *A* Why are you limping?

    B Because I fell and hurt my knee badly.

(*b*) Your passport is invalid since (*or* as) it expired on December 31st.

(*c*) *A* Why have you barred your windows like that?

    B For protection against burglars.

[71] Recommendation

(*a*) If you want really fresh fish, its best to get it at the market on Friday morning.

(*b*) You ought to see a dentist as soon as you can. Why not go to Mr Bay?

(*c*) What you need is a couple of weeks' rest by the sea. I should go somewhere quiet.

(*d*) The doctor recommended me to have a couple of weeks' rest by the sea.

[72] Reference

(*a*) Don't guess. Look up the word in the dictionary and make sure.

(*b*) Please refer to my letter of June 1st. You will find all the information there.

(*c*) With reference to your letter of June 10th, I should be grateful for further information on the following points.

(*d*) With regard to your final paragraph, I regret I have nothing to add.

(*e*) In applying for a post, please feel free to refer to your service with me. You may use my name as a reference (*or* I will gladly give you a reference).

[73]   Refusal

(*a*) No, I'm sorry but I can't let you use my typewriter.

(*b*) *A* May I leave a little early this afternoon, sir?
  B No, you may not.

(*c*) Mr and Mrs D. A. Smith thank Mr and Mrs Bacon for their kind invitation to a reception on July 14th, but regret they will be unable to attend (polite refusal).

(*d*) Marry you? My dear Jack, you must be out of your mind (one form of refusal of a proposal of marriage).

[74]   Regret

(*a*) I'm very sorry I said that. It was very foolish of me.

(*b*) In other words, I regret saying (*or* having said) that.

(*c*) Oh, but I so much wanted to see that play.

(*d*) Yes, I know, madam. But I regret to say that every seat is booked.

(*e*) See also [73] (*c*).

[75]   Repetition

(*a*) Madam, I've already explained that every seat is booked.

(*b*) Must I tell you again? You cannot use my typewriter (see [73] (*a*).

(*c*) The cheat! He copied every word, every single word, from my essay.

[76]   Request (for information)

(*a*) What is the time please? (rather abrupt).

(*b*) Can (*or* could) you tell me the time please? (more polite).

(*c*) Where is the post-office, please? (elementary and rather abrupt).

(*d*) Can (*or* could) you tell me the way to the post-office please? (more polite).

(*e*) Excuse me, where is the lavatory (*or* toilet), please?

(*f*) Can (*or* could) you tell me how to get to the railway station, please?

(*g*) Excuse me, is this the right way to Newmarket?

(*h*) Excuse me, am I on the right road for Cambridge?

(*i*) What does this word mean (please)?

(*j*) How do you spell your name, sir?

[77] Request (to buy, or borrow something)

(*a*) Can (*or* could *or* may *or* might) I have some of those apples, please?

(*b*) Can (*or* could *or* may *or* might) I borrow your pen for a moment?

(*c*) Lend me your pen for a moment (more familiar, expecting assent).

(*d*) Will (*or* would) you lend me your pen? *or* Lend me your pen, will you?

(*e*) Would you mind lending me your pen for a moment?

[78] Request (for action)

(*a*) Will you sit down? *or* Will you take a seat?

(*b*) Sit down, will you? *or* Take a seat will you? (not expecting a refusal).

(*c*) Would you mind closing that window? There's an awful draught.

(*d*) Might I trouble you to help me with this suitcase? It's too heavy for me.

[79] Right (in contrast to **Wrong**)

(*a*) You're quite right. Your answer was absolutely correct.

(*b*) You did quite right. The action you took was correct. You were right to take it.

(*c*) His story was true. It was borne out by the facts.

(*d*) It is only right that he should pay for the damage he caused.

[80] Size, see **Dimensions [26]**

[81] Space

(*a*) See **Dimensions [26]** (*c*).

(*b*) See **Location [43]** *in* (*my hand*).

(*c*) See **Motion [47]** into our *compartment, through tunnels*.

[82] Speed

(*a*) You're driving too fast. Please slow down.

(*b*) Light travels much faster than sound.

(*c*) Supersonic aircraft can fly at a thousand kilometres an hour.

(*d*) Money disappears like water these days. We shall be bankrupt at this rate.

[83]　State of Affairs

(*a*) Are you ill? You look very pale. Your voice sounds faint (current state).

(*b*) See **Change of State [16]**.

[84]　Suggestion

(*a*) Let's stop and have a look at those ruins, shall we?

(*b*) Shall we have our picnic under those trees and admire the view?

(*c*) I think it would be a good idea to eat now, don't you?

(*d*) We could drive on for another hour, if you like. I don't mind, it's only a suggestion.

[85]　Surface, see Dimension [26] (*e*) Location [43] and Motion [47]

[86]　Sympathy

(*a*) I'm sorry. What bad luck! And you had worked so hard for that examination.

(*b*) I'm so sorry to see you in this state. Don't worry about your work, and get well soon.

(*c*) I'm so sorry to hear about your wife. Do give her my very best wishes and I hope she makes a speedy recovery.

(*d*) I'm very, very sorry to hear about your brother. He was such a good man. Did he suffer very much?

(*e*) Please accept our deepest sympathy in your sad loss.

(*f*) Please accept our heartfelt condolences. (more formal).

[87]　Thankfulness

(*a*) Thank you very much for your letter of May 28th (normal beginning to a letter).

(*b*) Thank you so much for a most delightful evening (letter of thanks for hospitality).

(*c*) We are most grateful to you for your very generous donation.

(*d*) I should be grateful (*or* much obliged) if you would send me a sample of your material.

[88]　Time (measured in minutes, hours, days etc. See also Duration)

(*a*) At the third stroke, it will be twelve twenty-five precisely (recorded telephone message).

(*b*) *A* Do you have the time please?
　　B Yes, it's twelve twenty-five by my watch.

(*c*) *A* Is your watch right?
　　B Well, sometimes it's a little fast, sometimes a little slow.

(*d*) *A* When does the match start?

B It's due to start at three fifteen.

(*e*) *A* How long does it last?

B An hour and a half, plus a ten minute interval.

(*f*) *A* How long will it take us to get to Frankfurt?

B You can do it in two hours.

(*g*) It took the travellers four days to reach the coast *or* The travellers took four days to reach the coast.

[89] Time (*Present*)

(*a*) *Point of time* Watch me press this button, so, and the machine starts.

(*b*) *Period* My grandparents live in a cottage in the country now.

(*c*) *Habit* I do exercises for twenty minutes every day.

[90] Time (*Before Present*)

(*a*) *Pre-Present period ending, or continuing until, the present moment* We've just flown from Paris.

(*b*) *Pre-Present period, time of action unspecified* I've been to China.

(*c*) *Past, specified point of time* I went there in May.

(*d*) *Past, specified period* I learnt to swim when I was six.

[91] Time (*After Present*)

Emphasis on present conditions etc. leading to an expected future event or state:

(*a*) I'm going to Spain in July. (*Present intentions*).

(*b*) That tree is going to fall on our house one of these days (its present condition is so bad).

(*c*) We're having fish for supper (arrangements have already been made).

(*d*) I'm to be married in the morning (it's already planned).

(*e*) We leave for London at six o'clock this evening (according to schedule).

Emphasis on future time:

(*f*) My father will be seventy next December.

[92] Time (*referring to number of occurrences*)

(*a*) *A* I've been to Peking once.

B I've been there twice.

(*b*) *C* I've been there three times already.

(*c*) The moon goes round the earth thirteen times a year.

(*d*) You've said that twice. Please don't say it again (i.e. another time in the future).

(*e*) This is the first time our whole family have sat round the same table.

[93] Time (*point-of-time act*)

(*a*) e.g. *move*, *as in:* Since we moved here, we have made many friends.

(*b*) e.g. *leave*, *as in:* I want to leave by (i.e. not later than) seven o'clock.

[94] Time (*period-of-time, activity or state*)

(*a*) e.g. *live*, *as in:* Since we've lived (*or* been) here, we've made many friends.

(*b*) e.g. *wait*, *as in:* I'll wait here until eight o'clock.

(*c*) e.g. *not-leave*, *as in:* I'll not leave until eight o'clock.

[95] Value

(*a*) A Could you tell me how much these rings are worth, please?
  B This one is very valuable. It is solid gold and worth at least 500 dollars. The other one is only gold plated. It isn't exactly valueless, but it's worth very little.

(*b*) We are extremely grateful to you for your help. It has been invaluable (i.e. its value has been so great that it cannot be calculated).

[96] Volition (i.e. power to decide on and take a course of action)

(*a*) I will do all I can to help you, but I am not very happy about it.

(*b*) There is nothing for you to do. The Committee will decide what action to take.

[97] Warning

(*a*) Danger. Stop and make sure the line is clear before crossing.

(*b*) Be very careful as you go round the next bend. It's very dangerous.

(*c*) Poison. Not to be taken internally. Keep this bottle out of reach of children.

(*d*) Beware of splashes. They can do severe damage to eyes (notice on a vehicle carrying a chemical liquid).

[98] Willingness

(*a*) A Can I help you?
  B Yes please, if you will.

(*b*) *A* Will anyone volunteer to come with me?
   B We all will.
(*c*) *A* Will anyone drive Mrs Beeton to the station?
   B I will, gladly.

[99] **Wishes** (see **205** page 00)
   (*a*) When I was a little girl, I always wanted a doll like that.
   (*b*) If only we could get away and have no more worries!
   (*c*) Very best wishes for the New Year. With every good wish.
   (*d*) Best wishes. Very best wishes (typical endings of letters to friends or close business acquaintances).

[100] **Wrong**
   (*a*) Excuse me, but I think there is a mistake in my account.
   (b) I made no telephone calls, and, in any case, the addition is wrong.
   (*c*) I do apologise, sir. It was my mistake entirely.
   (d) If George said that, he is quite wrong. That story is completely untrue.
   (*e*) It would be wrong of me to punish him without hearing what he has to say.

APPENDIX

A. The 'solid core' (see 11) would include

(*a*) the basic rules of sentence structure, as exemplified in the patterns in Chapter 7; and the use of high-frequency verbs in the patterns appropriate to them. The patterns would include predicative adjectives and obligatory adverbials;

(*b*) rules for the pronunciation and spelling of regular noun plurals and of common irregular plurals;

(*c*) rules for the pronunciation, spelling and general use of the genitive with apostrophe *s*;

(*d*) personal pronouns;

(*e*) basic uses of determiners, e.g. *some*, *any*, etc., as noun-modifiers and pronouns;

(*f*) use of not-too-complex nominal groups, consisting of pre-modifiers (including attributive adjectives), head-words, and commonly used post-modifier constructions; e.g. *that big black car in the road*;

(*g*) indefinite pronouns, e.g. *something*;

(*h*) use of the imperative; Simple Present of verbs; and Simple Past of regular verbs; and forms of *be*, *have* and *do*;

(*i*) rules for the pronunciation and spelling of the 3rd person singular, Present tense; and of the *-ing* and *-ed* forms of regular verbs;

(*j*) concord of subject and verb, where appropriate;

(*k*) use of the 'phrasal verb' constructions;

(*l*) irregular verbs;

(*m*) primary uses of modals;

(*n*) basic use of progressive with appropriate verbs;

(*o*) basic use of Present and Past Perfect;

(*p*) the passive, with appropriate verb patterns;

(*q*) negation; Yes/No questions; and the various types of *Wh*-questions;

(*r*) basic uses of prepositions;

(*s*) adverbs, and adverb phrases, of manner, place, time and frequency;

(*t*) co-ordination; apposition;

(*u*) compound and complex sentences, with co-ordinate and sub-ordinate clauses, finite and non-finite.

The above is an inventory of important items. It is not supposed to reflect an order in which those items should be taught or learnt.

B. Books for further reading and reference

1 *Historical and Traditional*

A New English Grammar (Henry Sweet Oxford, Clarendon Press, 1891) 'intended to supply the want of a scientific English grammar' towards the close of the nineteenth century. This work opened the way for the more scientific grammars of the twentieth century, and is still valuable for background study.

Essential of English Grammar (Otto Jepsersen, Allen & Unwin, 1933) has proved popular for over forty years. It contains much important information, although many of its examples are taken from the English of earlier times.

A Handbook of English Grammar (R. W. Zandvoort, Longman, Seventh edition, 1975) provides a sound, academic description on lines that would now be generally regarded as 'traditional'.

2 *Less Advanced than 'English as a Foreign Language'*

A Reference Grammar for Students of English (R. A. Close, Longman, 1975) is both 'less advanced' and more comprehensive. It describes the English grammatical system as a whole and gives the kind of detailed information that students would want to find in a reference book.

A Guide to Patterns and Usage in English (A. S. Hornby, Oxford University Press, Second Edition, 1975) describes types of verb patterns, with plenty of examples. It discusses other aspects of English Grammar; and ends with a very useful chapter on 'Various Concepts and Ways they are expressed'.

3 *For Reference in company with 'English as a Foreign Language'*

The Oxford Advanced Learner's Dictionary of Current English (A. S. Hornby, Oxford University Press, Third Edition, 1974) besides giving clear definitions of meanings, labels most nouns as Countable or Uncountable and most verbs with symbols indicating in which patterns they are normally used.

The Longman Dictionary of Contemporary English (edited by Paul Proctor, Longman, 1977) besides giving clear definitions of meanings by using a controlled vocabulary, provides a more up-to-date analysis of verb patterns, and also indicates by symbols how adjectives and adverbs can be used.

The Oxford Dictionary of Idiomatic English, Volume 1 (A. P. Cowie and R. Mackin, Oxford University Press, 1975) concentrates on phrasal verbs, explaining what each means and giving examples in appropriate contexts.

4 *For a more academic, linguistic approach to English Grammar*

Grammar (Frank Palmer, Penguin Books, 1971) gives a brief introduction to modern linguistic thinking on the subject.

A Grammar of Contemporary English (R. Quirk, S. Greenbaum, G. Leech and J. Svartvik, Longman, 1972) has been described as 'the fullest and most comprehensive synchronic description of English grammar ever written'. This is a very advanced work, based on both traditional notions and on a thorough study of recent linguistic research.

A University Grammar of English (R. Quirk and S. Greenbaum, Longman, 1973) is a shorter version of the last mentioned work. It is accompanied by a *Workbook* (R. A. Close, Longman, 1974) designed to facilitate study of *A University Grammar* and to apply its principles and criteria by means of practical exercises.

The English Verb (F. R. Palmer, Longman, 1974) is a searching study of this important aspect of English Grammar.

Cohesion in English (M. A. K. Halliday and R. Hasan, Longman 1976) examines the grammatical and semantic links which bind sentences into a coherent and cohesive text.

5 *Meaning, Notions, Functions and Communication*

The short *Meaning and the English Verb* (G. Leech, Longman, 1971) deals specifically with the meaning of verb forms, particularly the Progressive and Perfective.

Working from meaning to form, rather than *vice versa*

A Communicative Grammar of English (G. Leech and J. Svartvik, Longman, 1975), summarises material from *A Grammar of Contemporary English*, mentioned above, but follows a communicative approach, i.e. it explains what grammatical devices English has for expressing basic notions, social aspects and personal attitudes.

Modern Languages: The Threshold Level (J. A. Van Ek, Council of Europe Committee for Cultural Development, Strasbourg, 1972) provides 'lists of concepts which the learner will be expected to be able to deal with in a foreign language' and discusses 'the level on which the learner has the ability to communicate' in particular situations.

Teaching Language as Communication (H. G. Widdowson, OUP 1978).

Notional Syllabuses (D. A. Wilkins, Oxford University Press, 1976) is a key work on this topic, discussing categories for a notional syllabus and ways in which such a syllabus might be applied.

INDEX

1. Individual words dealt with from a grammatical point of view are printed in italic. Grammatical terms and notions are in ordinary type.
2. Numbers refer to sections of the book—not to pages. Numbers in bold type refer to the principal treatment of the subject concerned.
3. adj. = adjective; adv. = adverb; det. = determiner; fn. = footnote; part. = particle; prep. = preposition; v = 'in contrast with'.

208